MODERN
FARMHOUSE
Made Easy

SIMPLE WAYS TO MIX OLD & NEW

CAROLINE McKENZIE

CENTENNIAL BOOKS

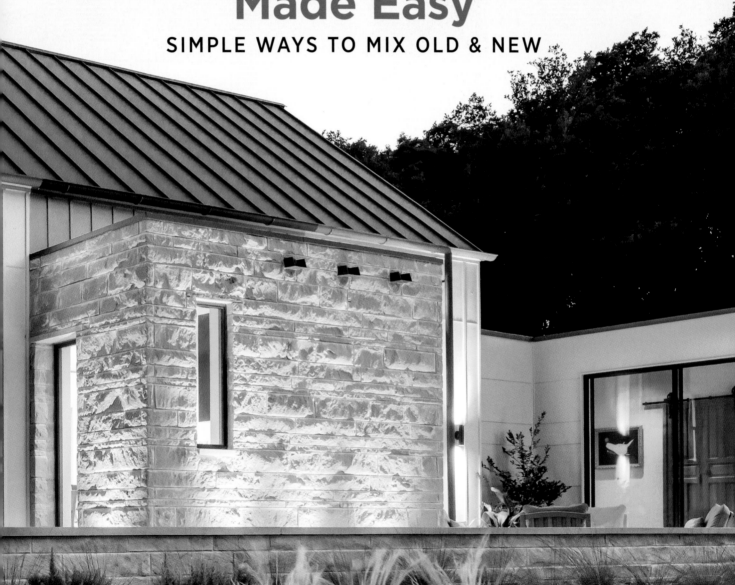

MODERN
FARMHOUSE
Made Easy

SIMPLE WAYS TO MIX OLD & NEW

70

contents

56

cultivate the look

16

come on in

make it yours

WELCOME
HOME

*The unpretentious appeal of modern farmhouses
is finding favor wherever you may roam.*

Farmhouses are having a moment. From coast to coast and now around the globe, people are shirking fussy décor in favor of a laid-back rustic-meets-industrial look. Characterized by natural textures and materials like iron, steel and galvanized metal, modern farmhouses serve up the best of both worlds with equal parts old-fashioned charm and sleek design. Contrasting elements—such as rough-hewn beams and glossy factory lights, for example—make happy companions that create eye-pleasing balance at every turn. Clean lines and patina mix seamlessly for rooms that exude warmth and simplicity.

It's safe to say that simplicity is integral to the appeal of the modern farmhouse movement. In a world of overbooked schedules, unending phone notifications, and too-long to-do lists, coming home to less-is-more style is nothing short of a breath of fresh air.

What's more, farmhouses are crowd-pleasers. And that's not just a nod to their current popularity: Beyond the shiplap and reclaimed beams, they offer warm, inviting rooms that inevitably make friends and family want to gather. Glitzier styles might leave guests (and even the homeowners) walking on eggshells for fear

of spoiling the swanky spaces. The farmhouse look celebrates objects and spaces designed to be lived in, not just looked at and admired. It's about rooms bursting with items with weather and wear that will, in turn, only gain appeal with more weather and wear. Farmhouses by their very nature are meant to take a beating. The current take on the style embraces that utilitarian tradition with designs that can withstand the messes of everyday life—kitchens where you can cook with abandon, living rooms where you don't have to worry about spills, mudrooms that can actually handle a pair of muddy boots.

Perhaps the real secret to the unwavering appeal of modern farmhouses is that the design is well-suited for virtually any location—not just the countryside. Indeed, you'd be hard-pressed to find a home that doesn't look better with a fresh mix of mod metals and soulful patina. From high-rises to cabins—it just works. Whether you own an honest-to-goodness farmhouse, live in a suburban new-build or are a city dweller looking to carve out a slice of the simple life, this book is here to inspire you to create casual, comfortable spaces with timeless, trend-proof style. It's warm, it's approachable and it's here to stay. You can bet the farm(house) on it.   —*Caroline McKenzie*

> **The farmhouse look celebrates objects and spaces designed to be lived in, not just looked at and admired."**

The modern farmhouse look is one of instant warmth and charm, a place you can sit down, settle back and feel at home.

7

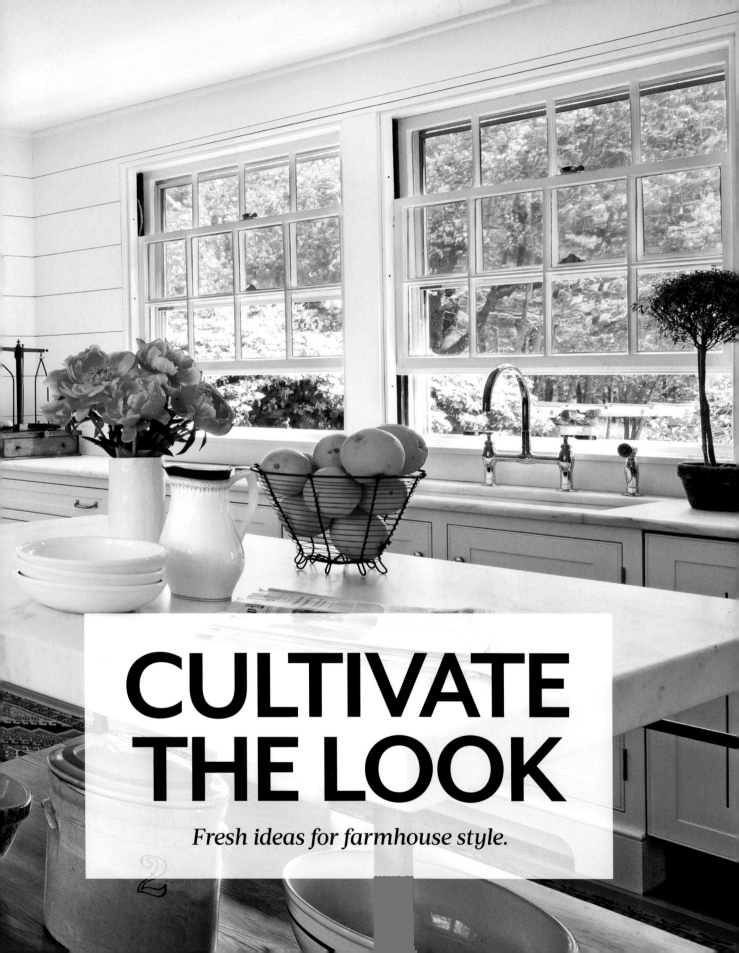

CULTIVATE THE LOOK

Fresh ideas for farmhouse style.

CURB APPEAL

FOR THE LOVE OF
WHITE FARMHOUSES

*They're classic for a reason! Try one of these
exterior paint colors to get your home beaming.*

FARMHOUSE FAVORITE
A MIX OF VERTICAL AND HORIZONTAL PANELING BRINGS TEXTURE TO THIS ALL-WHITE EXTERIOR.

All White
*by Farrow
& Ball*

ATHERTON, CALIFORNIA

5 bedrooms | 4.5 bathrooms
Designed by L'oro Designs

*Simply
White*
*by Benjamin
Moore*

NEWBURY,
MASSACHUSETTS

3 bedrooms | 2.5 bathrooms
Designed by Cummings Architects

STILLWATER, MINNESOTA
5 bedrooms | 4.5 bathrooms
Designed by Rehkamp Larson

DALLAS
3 bedrooms | 4 bathrooms
Designed by Jamie Olsen Ali and Demesne

TWO-OVER-TWO WINDOWPANES GIVE THE HOME A CLASSIC FINISH.

FRANKLIN, TENNESSEE
3 bedrooms | 3.5 bathrooms
Designed by J. Taylor Designs

White Heron
by Sherwin-Williams

ELLSWORTH, WISCONSIN
3 bedrooms | 2 bathrooms
Designed by SALA Architects

Super White
by Sherwin-Williams

Creamy
by Sherwin-Williams

AUSTIN, TEXAS
3 bedrooms | 2.5 bathrooms
Designed by Don Harris Architect
and Lori Smyth Design;
built by Mezger Homes

*CANDY-APPLE RED
MAKES FOR THE PERFECT
POP OF COLOR.*

Arctic White
by James Hardie Siding

LINCOLN, VERMONT
4 bedrooms | 2.5 bathrooms
Designed by MB Architecture + Design;
built by Hagstrom Builders

15

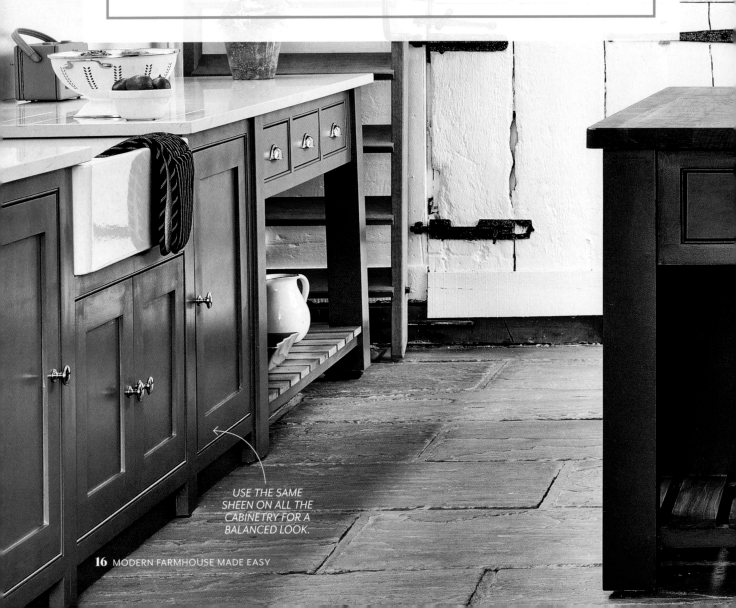

10 WAYS TO

COZY UP
YOUR KITCHEN

*Ensure the heart of the home also has plenty of soul
with these easy and undeniably charming ideas.*

USE THE SAME
SHEEN ON ALL THE
CABINETRY FOR A
BALANCED LOOK.

FARMHOUSE
FAVORITE
*EXPOSED
BLACK HINGES
OPEN THE DOOR TO
CLASSIC FARMHOUSE
PANACHE.*

No. 1
EMBRACE A SIGNATURE COLOR

Color can instantly zap a kitchen of a ho-hum, utilitarian feel. If you don't want to go all in with floor-to-ceiling cabinetry, consider coating an accent item, such as an island or built-in hutch, with a favorite shade.

EDITOR'S PICKS

Blue Nova
Benjamin Moore

New Mint Green
Glidden

Balmoral
Fine Paints of Europe

Calamine
Farrow & Ball

17

FARMHOUSE FAVORITE
WHITE SUBWAY TILES BRING A SLEEK (AND AFFORDABLE) ELEMENT TO A COUNTRY KITCHEN.

No. 2
GO RETRO

They don't make 'em like they used to. At least, that's the case when it comes to retro ranges, which can infuse an otherwise up-to-date cooking space with a heaping helping of old-school appeal. You can find the real deal at resources such as antiqueappliances.com or get the old look with new functionality from one of the many vendors churning out new takes on classic designs.

STYLE TIP
Look for a range in a vivid hue for even more charm.

No. 3
BRING THE OUTDOORS IN

Natural accents, such as fresh (or faux) flowers or cut branches give a kitchen an organic, at-one-with-nature quality. Bonus: They require zero commitment—and bring a dose of seasonality, to boot.

STYLE TIP
A trio of branches adds height, but without heft.

No. 4
SEE THE SIGNS

Even a plain-Jane kitchen can get an inviting makeover with the introduction of an antique sign. For an especially fitting accent, look for those sporting grocery and food references. And the more patina, the better!

STYLE TIP
Add a distressed frame to a reproduction sign for a convincingly vintage look.

STYLE TIP
Vintage brass lighting
will acquire an appealing
patina over time.

No. 5
LET THERE BE (SALVAGED) LIGHT

Sure, eye-catching lighting is a mainstay in kitchen designs. But what really cooks up some personality is unexpected, salvaged fixtures. In this space, for example, an antique chandelier casts a chic glow. Old factory or ship lighting brings an equally gleaming finish.

GLASS-FRONT CABINETS RECALL OLD GENERAL-STORE DISPLAYS.

STYLE TIP
Nothing to weigh?
Use it as a quaint spot
to store fruit or stash
phones and keys.

No. 6
PLAY THE SCALES

If you pick only one vintage piece to layer into your kitchen, let it be an old-fashioned scale. The pretty shape and color packs ample charm. (Not to mention, they're more food-safe than other antique kitchen items.)

No. 7
MAKE A (BACK)SPLASH

Whether crafted from porcelain, cement or even wood, a graphic tile design is like down-home jewelry for a kitchen. To avoid something overly modern, look to quilt-inspired motifs, which feel perfectly at home amid farmhouse décor.

STYLE TIP
A three-tone tile will pack in the color without appearing too busy.

No. 8
WARM WITH WOOD TONES

This modern kitchen casts a homey vibe, thanks to its repeated wood tones. Go for beefy beams or choose smaller-scale elements, such as old bread bowls and chopping boards.

STYLE TIP
Pre-fabricated faux beams are an easy alternative if you don't need load-bearing ones.

FARMHOUSE FAVORITE
WOOD TONES IN VARYING STAINS GIVE A SPACE A MORE RUSTIC AND COLLECTED LOOK.

No. 9
SHOW OFF A COLLECTION

Don't relegate a kitchen collection to a dusty cupboard. Instead, put it front and center with an out-in-the-open display that spotlights the beauty of everyday items.

STYLE TIP
Copper cookware is especially well-suited for farmhouse kitchens.

No. 10
SKIRT THE ISSUE

A skirted sink or cupboard brings a softness to a kitchen's many hard edges. It also provides an artful means of stashing less-than-eye-pleasing essentials. (Hello, worn-out frying pans.)

STYLE TIP
Ticking stripe is an affordable, country-approved fabric that hides stains.

23

DINING DETAILS

TABLE MATTERS

Whether your style is traditional, rustic, minimalist or cottage, dress up your sit-down space with easy-to-incorporate design ideas.

CLASSIC CANDLESTICK
WALL SCONCES CREATE
A TRADITIONAL VIBE.

TRADITIONAL

Get the Look With...

Oversize chandeliers in milky white

Elegant country blooms, such as hydrangeas or ranunculus

Handsome cutlery with wood-grain details

Glass goblets in classic shades of green or blue

RUSTIC

Get the Look With...

Chintz table linens with pretty shades of pink and red

An unexpected pop of glitzy sparkle

Humble serving pieces such as berry baskets or metal platters

Mismatched painted furniture—distressed finishes preferred!

COTTAGE

Get the Look With...

Red-and-white splatter ware—
an American classic!

Quaint
Windsor
chairs

Striped linens that can
double as dish cloths

Understated
task lighting in
place of a fussy
chandelier

MINIMALIST

Get the Look With...

Simple succulents
in lieu of fussy
centerpieces

Mod botanical prints for
napkins or place mats (no
tablecloths here!)

A mix of midcentury
and factory-style
seating

Simple, Scandinavian-inspired dinnerware

OPEN SHELVING
AND BRIGHT
BRASS POTS
BRING FORTH THE
COTTAGE FEEL.

**FARMHOUSE
FAVORITE**
*RED-AND-WHITE
DINNERWARE IS
COME-AS-YOU-ARE
COTTAGE STYLE
AT ITS BEST.*

ON DISPLAY

COLLECTIVE
CONSCIOUSNESS

*Is it really a farmhouse without a collection
or two? Start gathering some of these timeless
pieces to fill your home with storied style.*

EARTHENWARE PITCHERS
Glazed earthenware pitchers in soft
shades of cream, blue and green bring
softness to a space. Use them as planters
and vases throughout your house,
or simply group them in abundance.

VINTAGE CLOCKS

Midcentury windup alarm clocks wake up sleepy shelves with a bit of quirkiness. (Tip: When looking for them on large online sites such as Etsy, try searching "Big Ben" clock.)

KITCHEN TINS

Antique food tins (from coffee, cookies, chips, etc.) recall a time when thoughtful packaging was the norm. They're relatively affordable collectibles ($15–$30 per tin), but expect those featuring dogs to fetch a higher rate.

WOVEN BASKETS

Baskets make for a textured display that can easily be taken down from the wall for everyday use. Look for items with similar depth for a cohesive vignette.

FARMHOUSE FAVORITE
VINTAGE OIL PORTRAITS (OFTEN FOUND AT ESTATE SALES) PAIR WELL WITH WEATHERED COLLECTIONS.

IRONSTONE

Developed in 19th-century England as a cheaper alternative to porcelain, ironstone is now coveted in its own right. Prized for their heavy weight and creamy finish, individual pieces often sell for $100 each.

TEACUPS

Colorful teacups bring feminine whimsy to a space—and can often be scooped up for less than $5 apiece. Display them in an old mail sorter, like the one shown here, for a vignette equally steeped in elegance and rusticity.

BLUE-AND-WHITE CHINA

The old (sometimes ancient) motifs found on blue-and-white china give it a timeless appeal. Mix restaurant-grade pieces with actual antiques for a robust grouping that doesn't break the bank.

FLORAL PAINTINGS

These thrift-shop staples may look shabby solo—but displayed as a group, they grow to chic new heights. Look for signed pieces to differentiate paintings from prints.

COME ON IN

Tours of real-life farmhouses.

FARMHOUSE FAVORITE
METAL ROOFING BRINGS SHARP LINES AND AMPLE DURABILITY.

MODERN STEEL WINDOWS ADD EDGE AGAINST CLASSIC SIDING.

UP ON TOP
A mix of materials and rooflines creates the impression that the house evolved over time rather than happening in one fell swoop.

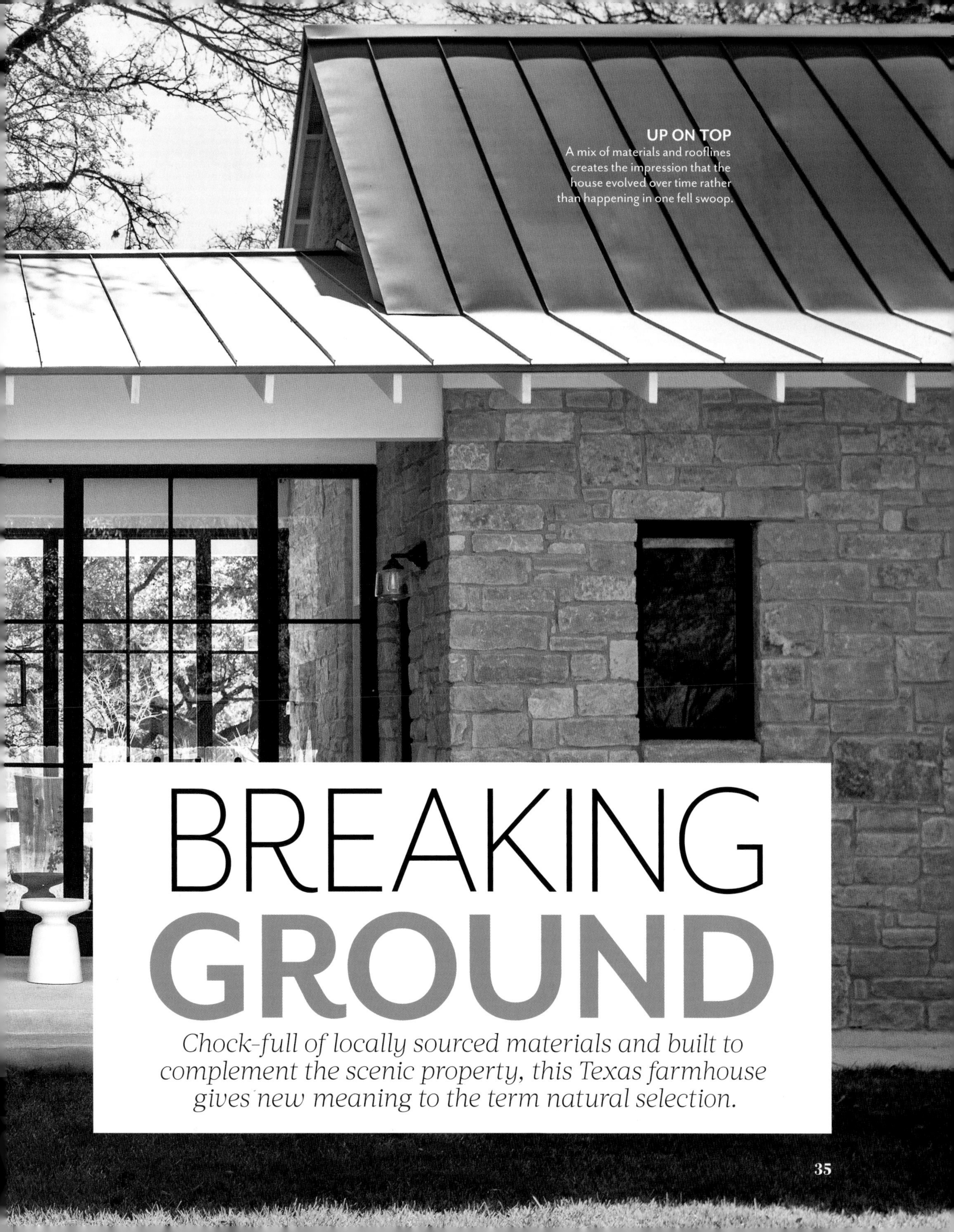

BREAKING GROUND

Chock-full of locally sourced materials and built to complement the scenic property, this Texas farmhouse gives new meaning to the term natural selection.

Architecture may call for buildings that cover up the land. But for Austin, Texas–based Tim Cuppett, it's the lay of the land that truly guides his work. "At the start of every project, I walk the property and let it speak to me," he explains. "The views and the light are inspiration." And so, when clients came to him looking to build a forever home on a large lot just outside of town, the first thing Cuppett did was take a field trip. "There was one spot, tucked underneath live oaks. It just felt like if you were going to hang out on the property—even without a house—this is where you'd want to be," he recalls. The building site selected, he hit the ground running, so to speak, with a design that took inspiration from the locale—using locally sourced materials, including walnut flooring and limestone masonry, and plenty of expansive windows to show off the surrounding vistas. The latter were thoughtfully planned so that every room in the home benefits from natural light on

ARRANGING BOOKS BY TOPIC, RATHER THAN COLOR, CREATES A LIBRARY FEEL.

▲
OLD MEETS NEW
Expanses of glass and a vibrant turquoise front door liven up the classic design elements.

BRIGHT THIS WAY

Cuppett meticulously designed the laid-back living room so that natural light pours in from all four directions. An "interior" window along the stairwell does the trick on the far end of the room. "There's a window at the top of the stair landing. I desperately wanted that light to come down and penetrate not only the kitchen but also the living room," he explains. A built-in bookshelf, piled with colorful tomes, and an olive-green midcentury recliner, up the room's cozy factor.

FARMHOUSE FAVORITE *WIDE-PLANK FLOORS IN A DARK STAIN WILL ONLY LOOK BETTER WITH AGE.*

V-GROOVE PANELING MATCHES THE TEXTURE OF THE STONE WALLS.

FIRST IMPRESSIONS

Not wanting the home's overall footprint to be too expansive, Cuppett tucked the dining room into a handsome stone-and-glass-encased pass-through that connects the garage and main living area. "Dining rooms tend to be pretty, streamlined spaces," he explains. "This felt like the right way to welcome guests without a traditional foyer."

FARMHOUSE FAVORITE
SCONCES LEND A FACTORY FEEL—IT'S FAR MORE STORIED THAN THE EFFECT OF CAN LIGHTING.

WINDOWS ON THE WORLD

The kitchen is "all about the windows," says Cuppett, who cites it as having the best views in the house. To maximize them, he forwent upper cabinetry. There's still plenty of storage, thanks to the open shelving that spans the length of the windows.

FARMHOUSE FAVORITE
A BARN DOOR IS A PASTORAL AND SPACE-EFFICIENT ELEMENT IN A MASTER SUITE.

PUT IT IN NEUTRAL

The master bedroom's palette of gray and ochre is intentionally neutral, keeping the focus on what's beyond the windows. Textured accents, such as woven baskets, linen curtains and a cowhide rug (made of small hexagon pieces that are more affordable than a single hide), prevent a one-note look.

TUB TIME

A single element can infuse a space with farmhouse charm. In the master bathroom, for example, an old-fashioned tub with extra-chunky claw feet does the trick.

at least two sides. (Impressively, the living room laps it up in all four directions.)

Also central to the design: scale. "I didn't want to detract from the natural topography, including all those oaks," Cuppett explains. "Likewise, I wanted it to feel like an authentic farmhouse, which would have had comfortable, but not colossal, rooms." As a result, the majority of the home is only one room wide.

Cuppett, who is also an interior designer, then worked with the family to furnish the house with minimalist pieces that once again keep the focus on the outdoors. The result is a family-friendly abode where the clients feel as much at home as the house feels on the land. Leave it to him to create a natural fit. ■

▼

CENTRAL LOCATION

The novel staircase leads straight into the kitchen and living room so the rooms feel connected without a too-open floor plan. "There's a playroom at the top of the stairs—the family can call to one another," Cuppett says.

> 66
> We kept rooms moderately sized so the spaces could take in plenty of natural light and feel true to the proportions of an old farmhouse."
>
> TIM CUPPETT

41

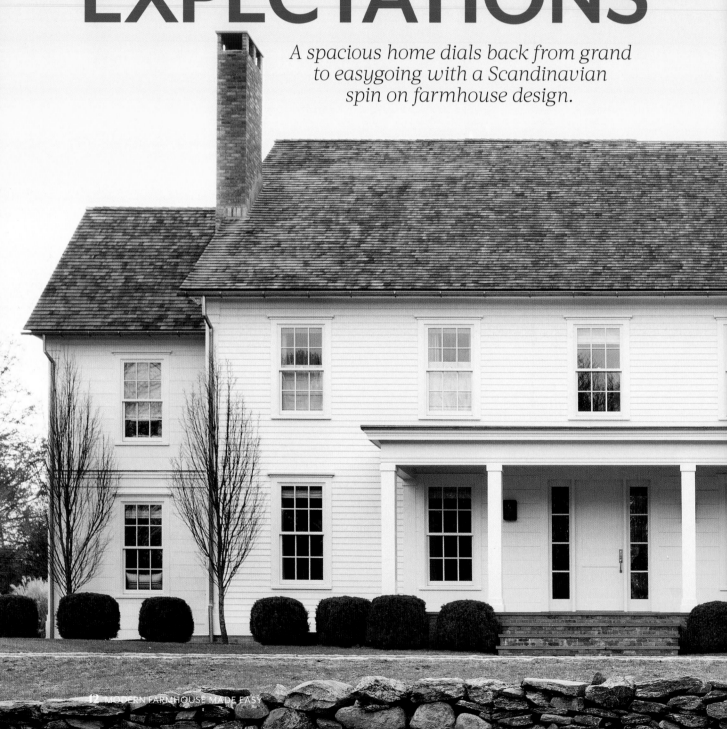

GREAT EXPECTATIONS

A spacious home dials back from grand to easygoing with a Scandinavian spin on farmhouse design.

FARMHOUSE FAVORITE
AN ALL-WHITE EXTERIOR BRINGS COUNTRY STYLE IN SPADES.

PERFECT HARMONY
If you look closely, you can spot the thin cladding that separates the central, original portion of the home from the new wings flanking the left and right. The cedar siding was put through a rigorous aging process to more closely replicate the real deal.

NATURAL LIGHT FLOWS THROUGHOUT THE HOUSE, LENDING A BRIGHT AND AIRY FEEL.

METAL RIVETS GIVE THE DEN DISCREET INDUSTRIAL ACCENTS.

Susanna Simonpietri, creative director at the Brooklyn-based design firm Chango & Co., had never tackled a farmhouse. But you wouldn't know that from the looks of the Westport, Connecticut, home she brought to life for her clients. The old home had recently been flipped by a local contractor, with additions added to both sides. "When I was pulled into the project, most of the finishes, flooring, tile and so forth were already in place. It was lovely but a bit formal for a young family. The minute I stepped inside, I knew a modern interpretation of 'farmhouse' was what it needed to go from merely pretty to inviting." A longtime aficionado of Scandinavian design, Simonpietri studied the aesthetic closely, pulling in hallmarks of the look—the

▶

CURRENT AFFAIRS
Part of Simonpietri's secret to creating an old-fashioned home that feels fresh? Just enough modern furniture and fixtures (like the black metal sconces) to prevent the home from veering into museum territory.

FARMHOUSE FAVORITE
BUILT-INS WITH METAL FRETWORK PANELS CALL TO MIND CUPBOARDS OF YORE.

45

GRAY MATTER

Gray and off-white quite literally
water down the more classic and
expected combo of black and
white for a softer, subtler space.

> **"**We wanted the colors to be a bit milky and soft, just so the house felt a little more relaxed."
>
> SUSANNA SIMONPIETRI

HANGING A MIRROR FROM AN OLD BARN HOOK CREATES A STABLE VIBE.

FARMHOUSE FAVORITE
METAL LIGHTING FINISHES THE LOOK WITH UTILITARIAN FLAIR.

wood tones, simple accessories and light, muted colors—to churn out her own take on modern farmhouse style. Those muted colors were especially integral in creating spaces that felt in keeping with the grandness of the home while staying approachable. "We wanted the colors to be a bit milky and soft, just so the house felt a little more relaxed," she explains. That softness was also repeated in the home's weatherworn antiques, many of which were handpicked by Simonpietri herself. "Let's just say that when I go to market, I go prepared to do some digging. I wear pants I don't mind getting ruined among dirty antiques."

With each room now wonderfully appointed and the clients pleased as punch, it's safe to say her first time out was more than beginner's luck. ∎

◄

TAKE THE EDGE OFF
With its custom built-ins and millwork, the living room had good bones from the get-go. All Simonpietri needed to do was take the cozy quotient up a notch. She did so with the introduction of a duo of white canvas sofas and an extra-nubby grass cloth wallpaper.

THE BUILT-INS WERE PAINTED TAUPE TO BETTER MESH WITH THE WALLPAPER.

FARMHOUSE FAVORITE
AN ALL-WHITE KITCHEN NEVER FAILS TO READ AS CLASSIC.

THIS SMART COMBO PAIRS GLASS-FRONT CABINETS WITH OPEN SHELVES.

DREAM WEAVER

Sometimes all a space needs is a cozy spot to perch on. In the kitchen, for example, Simonpietri introduced woven barstools that are not only incredibly comfortable, with low-slung curvy backs, but also bring warm texture into the all-white room.

BALANCE BEAMS
The common farmhouse trope is rustic, raw-wood beams. Pretty as that may be, Simonpietri intensified the sophistication (and softness) by coating this home's exposed woodwork in high-gloss hues.

FARMHOUSE FAVORITE *BOTANICAL PRINTS AND PHOTOGRAPHS EVOKE ICONIC RURAL LANDSCAPES.*

LINGER ON

Comfort was a priority at every turn—even in the formal dining room, where leather Parsons chairs stuffed with goose down are cozy enough "to sit for hours and not want to get up," says Simonpietri.

SOFT-SERVE

In the master bedroom, a grass cloth wall covering, a plush area rug and upholstered furnishings make the entire room feel as though it's wrapped up in a big blanket.

A WOVEN COT IS A VERSATILE PIECE THAT CAN BE DRESSED UP (OR DOWN) WITH PILLOWS.

FARMHOUSE FAVORITE
LACE IS AN OLD-FASHIONED DETAIL THAT FEELS FRESH WHEN USED SPARINGLY.

▼
LADY-IN-WAITING
The neutral palette takes a feminine turn in the master bathroom, where peachy-pink walls and lace-lined curtains pour on ladylike poise. Polished nickel fixtures and an oversize mirror finish the jewel-box effect.

A STREAMLINED SOAKING TUB IS AS ELEGANT AS ITS CLAW-FOOTED COUNTERPART.

55

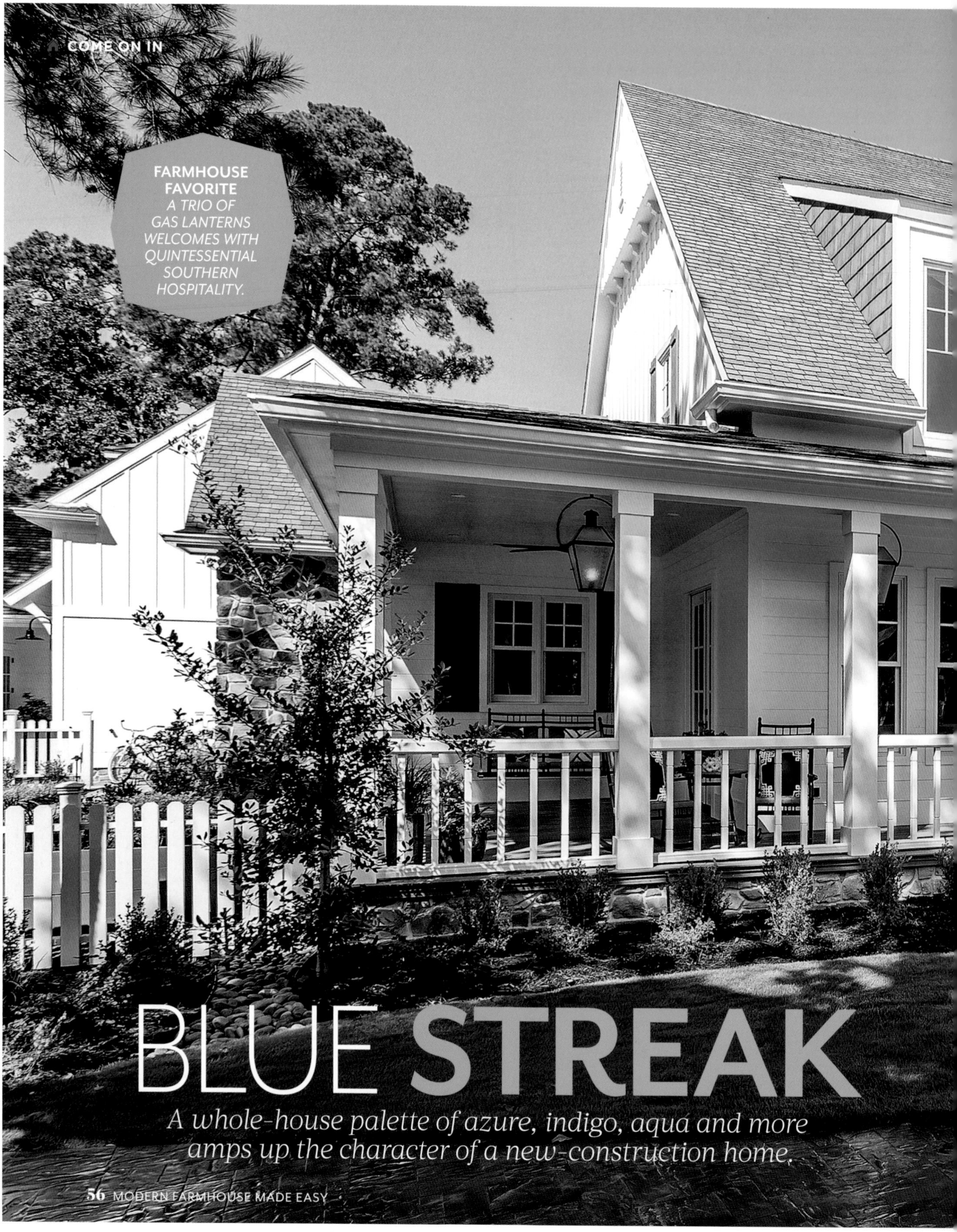

FARMHOUSE FAVORITE
A TRIO OF GAS LANTERNS WELCOMES WITH QUINTESSENTIAL SOUTHERN HOSPITALITY.

BLUE STREAK

A whole-house palette of azure, indigo, aqua and more amps up the character of a new-construction home.

STONE'S THROW
A stone facade gives the
new build timeless appeal
that's rock-solid.

RISE TO THE OCCASION
It doesn't get more classic than an L-shaped staircase, with the newel posts and railings finished in a high-contrast ebony stain.

Step inside the stately entrance of this Texas home, and you might get the feeling it's been around for generations. But you'd be fooled. It's actually a new build, co-designed by Texas-based Morning Star Builders and Chairma Design Group. And yes, their trickery is entirely intentional. Blessed with a gloriously flat lot—along a prized golf course, no less—the team decided to model the house, which started as a spec-home project, after a classic Southern farmhouse. "Golf course homes tend to go trendy or

SPLENDOR IN THE GRASS
The builders steered clear of an ornate facade in favor of a farmhouse look alongside the scenic Southern golf course.

QUILT TO LAST
A custom entryway rug (pieced together from rug samples) provides an affordable floor covering that also winks at a country-quilt design.

FARMHOUSE FAVORITE
LARGE POTTED PLANTS BRING A TOUCH OF THE OUTDOORS INSIDE AND BLEND PERFECTLY INTO ANY ROOM.

WRAPPING A RANGE HOOD IN SHIPLAP ACCENTUATES THE RUSTIC DÉCOR.

FARMHOUSE FAVORITE
LARGE POTTED PLANTS BRING A TOUCH OF THE OUTDOORS INSIDE AND BLEND PERFECTLY INTO ANY ROOM.

ornate—or both," says Cindy Aplanalp-Yates, the principal designer at Chairma. "We wanted something upscale and befitting the locale but that would also give the impression it's been around for years."

What they landed on was a 7,000-square-foot house showcasing numerous elements of the Southern farmhouse aesthetic, including sprawling porches, shiplap paneling and barn doors. While the architecture is rooted in the past, the home is far from staid. Throughout, there are numerous references to the color blue, an endlessly versatile color that bridges the gap between current and classic. "The home's many pops of blue—from bright aqua to moody navy—do a lot to enliven the space," says Aplanalp-Yates. "They bring in a scheme that won't soon tire, and also take the edge off the new architectural elements." The end result is a spec home that is, in a word, spectacular. ∎

MINI BENCHES AND TABLES MAKE IT EASY TO CUSTOMIZE THE LIVING SPACE.

◄
EASY DOES IT
The sunny family room offers plenty of seating, with bright, fun fabrics and cozy textures. (The easy-to-clean textiles ensure all ages feel at home in the space!)

*AN ORB CHANDELIER
ECHOES THE
CIRCULAR SEATING
ARRANGEMENT.*

**FARMHOUSE
FAVORITE**
*MEANDERING FLORAL
CURTAINS GIVE
ROOMS A VERTICAL-
GARDEN EFFECT.*

CHAIR AND CHAIR ALIKE
The house features an old-fashioned keeping room (shown here and at left). The radial seating arrangement (including four cushy armchairs!) and soothing blue walls are equally suited to after-dinner chatter and afternoon naps.

GLASS PENDANTS CAST FLATTERING LIGHT WITHOUT OBSCURING THE VIEW.

FARMHOUSE FAVORITE
A FEED-A-CROWD DINING TABLE IS THE IDEAL FINISH TO ANY COUNTRY KITCHEN.

ISLAND TIME
Yellow, blue's longtime country companion, takes a starring turn in the kitchen, where the happy hue envelops the expansive island. Adding to the cheery look is a host of patterns and textures, including a block-print window valance, a white-oak ceiling, a shiplap range hood and two different backsplash materials (pressed tin and white subway tile).

GREAT BLUE YONDER

This room-with-a-view's inviting palette of aquas, grays and crisp white is as happy as it is relaxing. Adding to that ambiance is the artful ceiling, where the dazzling wall color continues between custom coffered beams.

FARMHOUSE FAVORITE
NARROW, ABOVE-THE-CABINET WINDOWS RESEMBLE OLD-FASHIONED TRANSOMS.

Blue conveys a sense of calm, peacefulness and relaxation in all of its many shades and tones.

A GLASS ENCLOSURE SEPARATES THE TUB AND SHOWER WITHOUT BLOCKING SUNLIGHT.

CLEAN CUT
The barn doors alone (opposite page) are enough to give this master bath some serious cool factor. But just beyond, there's also a modern "wet room," with the tub and shower separated from the rest of the bathroom by glass, maximizing light and efficiency.

FARMHOUSE FAVORITE
ABSTRACT LANDSCAPES PROVE EQUAL PARTS PASTORAL AND MOD.

RUBBED BRONZE PROVIDES RUST-RESISTANT OUTDOOR HARDWARE.

PORCH ON THE CHARM

The farmhouse vibe continues to the covered back porch, where a custom barn door, painted a steely shade of blue-gray, slides open to reveal an equally handsome kitchenette.

IN THE WASH
The laundry room showcases yet another shade of blue, this time a blue-gray iteration that adds depth without detracting from the graphic hexagon tiles. A folk-art dog sculpture oversees the fetching look.

LIVING ROOM
What's Rustic A textured post-and-beam design, as well as caramel-hued leather chairs
What's Industrial Gleaming black lighting and streamlined furniture, like the armless sofa
A menswear-inspired color palette of gray, blue, black and white

TRUE
GRIT
This home in New York's Hamptons skips nautical motifs and preppy panache in favor of a rugged vibe.

Interior designer Timothy Godbold's marching orders were anything but simple: "Create a Hamptons beach house that feels nothing like a Hamptons beach house." The clients wanted a home that was sleek, but also inviting, and not a carbon copy of the often-opulent homes that dominate the area. While some designers might have hemmed and hawed over a direction, Godbold had a clear vision from the start. "The clean lines and warm finishes of a modern farmhouse made perfect sense," he explains. "It's on the coast, but the house is

ARCHITECTURAL
SALVAGE
CONTRASTS
WITH MODERN
ARTWORK.

OVERSIZE PENDANT LIGHTING HELPS TO DEFINE THE DINING AREA IN THE OPEN SETTING.

FARMHOUSE FAVORITE
TRESTLE TABLES LEND A SCULPTURAL ELEMENT TO A ROOM.

surrounded by lush fields. The look feels right at home." To ensure the project didn't go too country kitsch or too unapproachably modern, Godbold looked to a design recipe of rustic, industrial and refined elements throughout the home. Here, a room-by-room guide to how he put that no-fail formula into action. ∎

DINING ROOM
What's Rustic Leather dining chairs with hand-stitched cushions; the honey-hued wood tabletop
What's Industrial The metal-clad table base, as well as the iron framework found on the dining chairs
What's Refined The subtle pops of blue and orange underfoot; the voluminous pendants that add billowy scale

ENTRYWAY
What's Rustic A dark-stained trestle console table
What's Industrial Factory remnants (including the framed molds), and the print featuring a raven encased in scaffolding
What's Refined The black slate floor and the lush floral arrangement

73

A SHIPYARD-INSPIRED LIGHT PAYS HOMAGE TO THE BEACH LOCATION.

KITCHEN & WET BAR

What's Rustic Wide-plank whitewashed oak floors and floating shelves crafted from the same material **What's Industrial** In the kitchen, moody blue cabinetry that takes its color cue from metal factory storage; a concrete countertop in the wet bar **What's Refined** Elongated subway tile (measuring 12 inches long versus the standard 6) and slim brass cabinet hardware

RICH BLACK STAIN POPS AGAINST WHITE WALLS.

" The clean lines of a modern farmhouse made perfect sense."

TIMOTHY GODBOLD

75

READING NOOK

What's Rustic The mounted antelope antlers; the striped bedding inspired by a classic grain-sack motif
What's Industrial The metal daybed (actually a shortened full-size bed, so it is deeper than normal) and svelte task lighting
What's Refined A crisp black-and-white color scheme. Also, curvy accents, like the black and crystal-encrusted mirrors

SLIM LAMPS CAST A GLOW WITHOUT TAKING UP TOO MUCH SPACE.

FARMHOUSE FAVORITE
SHADOW BOXES PROVIDE AN ARTFUL MEANS OF DISPLAYING TREASURES.

◀

STUDY

What's **Rustic** Throw pillows with a graphic Aztec motif; touches of leather; raw-wood open shelves

What's **Industrial** Streamlined furniture in gleaming black, as well as the duo of task lamps

What's **Refined** Pops of green by way of the potted succulents

WIRE SHELVING KEEPS ITEMS IN PLAIN SIGHT.

SKIPPING A FRAME CREATES A MORE RELAXED LOOK.

77

> The house is on the coast, but is surrounded by lush fields. The farmhouse look is right at home."
> TIMOTHY GODBOLD

A NEUTRAL PALETTE KEEPS THE FOCUS ON THE OUTDOORS.

MASTER BEDROOM

What's Rustic Vaulted beams that continue to the second-floor master suite; expansive doors that open to the fields beyond
What's Industrial A clean-lined metal canopy bed (wrapped in leather)
What's Refined A subdued tone-on-tone color scheme; handsome armchairs

A CANOPY BED BALANCES THE TALL CEILINGS.

MASTER BATHROOM

What's Rustic The cerused-wood vanity and bovine print

What's Industrial Oil-rubbed bronze faucets and fixtures, including wall hooks; a trio of zinc sconces above the vanity

What's Refined White subway tile on the walls; black-and-white basket weave tile on the floor: both timeless

79

GUEST BEDROOM

What's Rustic Anchoring raw wood pieces
—from the room's bed to its beams
What's Industrial The lamp's matte black
finish mimics the look of old pipe fittings
What's Refined Black-and-white mohair
pillows with delicate fringe finish the tailored
bed linens

> Per the clients' request, it's a Hamptons beach house that feels nothing like a Hamptons beach house."
>
> TIMOTHY GODBOLD

KIDS' ROOMS

What's Rustic Arrow-print wallpaper (left); a cheeky dog portrait (below); artwork painted on wood planks (right)
What's Industrial A steel canopy bed with a deconstructed silhouette (left); metal sconces instead of bedside lamps (right)
What's Refined Simple bed linens in ticking and cabana stripes; a classic Jenny Lind spindle crib

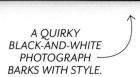

*A QUIRKY
BLACK-AND-WHITE
PHOTOGRAPH
BARKS WITH STYLE.*

A FLOATING
BOOKSHELF KEEPS
FLOOR SPACE
CLEAR.

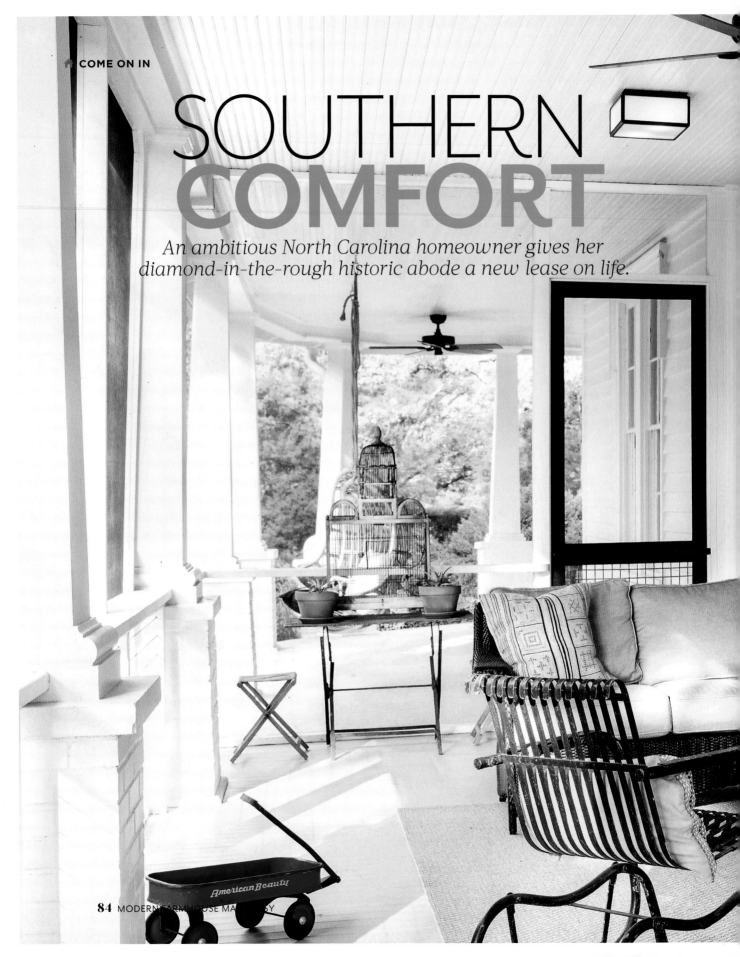

SOUTHERN
COMFORT

An ambitious North Carolina homeowner gives her diamond-in-the-rough historic abode a new lease on life.

PARLOR-LIKE PORCH

Inspired by her time spent on porches at her grandparents' homes in the South, homeowner Alys Protzman equipped her spacious wraparound with classics including wicker, rattan and tobacco baskets. Together, they create an outdoor parlor vibe that's as inviting as it was back in the good ol' days.

▲
CLASSIC EXTERIOR
The circa-1880s home sits on
23 acres just outside the Chapel Hill
city limits. Drawn to its historic bones,
Alys left the front of the home virtually
untouched—save for a fresh coat of paint
(Exterior White by Sherwin-Williams).

A s an interior designer in Chapel Hill, North
Carolina, Alys Protzman, owner of the firm
Alys Design, has worked with her share of
ritzy homes. (Think grass cloth, lacquer and
crystal chandeliers.) But when it came to
her own house, she was looking for something far more
relaxed. Enter a circa-1880s farmhouse on 23 rolling
acres just outside the city limits. "We wanted flowers and
vegetable gardens and bonfires—we knew this was our
chance at a farm life," she explains.

Though the property was a dream find for Alys and her
husband, Alex, it was a giant undertaking for the first-time
home buyers. Numerous nuts-and-bolts items needed
attention, including updating the electrical work and
replacing the radiant heat with a new central air unit. The
couple also decided to move forward with an expansive

▲
EXPANSIVE BREEZEWAY
When working to pin down details of the renovation, Alys was
a stickler about one element: the hallway. The home retained
an extra-wide hallway that stretched from the front door to
the back (meant to catch cross breezes way back when), and
she planned to keep it that way. "I love seeing all the way
through the house the minute you walk in the front door," she
explains. "The home just wouldn't be the same without it."

The house is all about reflecting our personal style.
We used texture and materials and artwork to tell our story."

ALYS PROTZMAN

" We wanted flowers and vegetable gardens and bonfires—we knew this was our chance at a farm life."

ALYS PROTZMAN

◀

BOLD POPS OF COLOR

Stealing the show in the living room is an original painting by Australian artist Allyson Reynolds. The colorful commission features oversize moths—a nod to the house's locale. ("We're surrounded by bugs out here!" says Alys.) To keep the large piece from feeling too grand, she leaned it against the wall above the mantel for a more casual look.

MARBLE COUNTERTOPS GLEAM AMID RUSTIC FINISHES LIKE THIS RANGE HOOD.

addition that brought a more open floor plan and natural light to the rear of the home. "We were planning to start a family, and an updated layout just made sense," she explains.

The renovation to-do list was nearly as long as the house was old, but Alys found herself loving every minute. "As an interior designer, this was sort of a dream project for me," she says. "I'd always envisioned living in an old house

and was ready for the hard work it takes to bring one back to top form."

During the renovation, Alys uncovered a wealth of hidden gems, including original heart-of-pine flooring beneath the black-and-white linoleum that dominated the downstairs. The discovery led her to use the traditional Southern hardwood on accents throughout the home, including the kitchen's statement-making range hood.

TEXTURED KITCHEN

Alys' rustic-meets-modern aesthetic is best on display in the kitchen, where rough-hewn elements—a heart pine range hood; a brick backsplash—are paired with sleek cabinets and marble countertops.

BESPOKE FURNISHINGS

Alys was blessed with a wealth of hand-me-down furniture but decided to chart her own course in the breakfast nook. There, classic leather Cab chairs (an investment that will only look better with age) surround a table crafted by her husband, Alex.

FARMHOUSE FAVORITE
FACTORY STOOLS LEND INDUSTRIAL EDGE TO A ROOM.

GLASS AND METAL PENDANTS GIVE A MODERN VIBE.

SERENE ESCAPE

"Tree house" was the vibe Alys wanted in her newly renovated master bedroom. To achieve the look, she incorporated vaulted ceilings (with hand-hewn beams), large windows (with minimal draperies) and a decidedly neutral palette (with plenty of texture). Rounding out the design is a sleek Scandinavian potbelly stove by Jøtul.

> 66
> ## I'd always envisioned living in an old house, and was ready for the hard work it takes to bring one back to top form."
>
> ALYS PROTZMAN

FARMHOUSE FAVORITE
AZTEC-INSPIRED TEXTILES OFFER UP WESTERN FLAIR.

HAND-HEWN RAFTERS INFUSE THE ROOM WITH ORGANIC TEXTURE.

"I wanted to preserve as much of the original architecture as we could. I looked to texture and materials to tell the story of a historic home," Alys adds.

While she was all for rustic accents, she was also careful to avoid anything overtly country. "I didn't want it to be all old signs and chicken wire," Alys explains. From the beginning, she envisioned punches of color and elements of modernity. To achieve that look, she painted the refurbished interior a creamy shade of white (White Dove by Benjamin Moore) and looked to bright artwork and accents to liven up the look.

With the renovation now a distant memory ("Totally worth it," she says) and the house chock-full of her sunny style, Alys' former diamond in the rough is shining brighter than ever. ■

HARDWORKING ACCENTS
Spare wood from the kitchen's range hood were used to craft shelves above each of the master bath sinks.

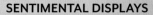

FARMHOUSE FAVORITE
CHIPPY FURNITURE, LIKE THIS ANTIQUE BENCH, ADDS HISTORY TO A HOME.

SENTIMENTAL DISPLAYS

Here's to unconventional artwork! To the right of the bench is a framed copy of an old *Life* magazine. To the left, a portion of the farmhouse's original hand-blocked wallpaper is visible. Alys discovered it during the renovation and chose to leave this portion unpainted. Her husband crafted a frame to perfectly encase the historic find.

STRIKING MUDROOM

The mudroom floor features bricks Alys found discarded on the property. (Her handyman cut them in half so they'd be paver depth.) The shiplap walls and bevy of natural wood tones ensure the hardworking spot is also a stylish one.

A THRIFT STORE SIDE TABLE GETS NEW LIFE AS A WORKBENCH.

CORRUGATED METAL SIDING IS DURABLE AND EASY TO MAINTAIN—JUST HOSE IT DOWN!

FOR KEEPS

This Austin dwelling merges novel architecture and a handsome Texas aesthetic into a house with staying power.

Some people want it all. Eric Rauser's client wasn't one of them. The Austin–based architect, who works for Risinger & Co. (the firm also constructed the home), was asked by a discerning homeowner to build a place where simplicity and efficiency were the top priorities. "The idea of a home rooted in the Texas farmhouse vernacular, but utilizing modern building techniques, instantly came to mind," says Rauser, who decided to implement a new construction concept, originated by Dr. Joe Lstiburek of Building Science Corp., that places the insulation on the outside of the home. "The result is an energy-efficient and incredibly durable structure," says Rauser. "This house is

97

SIT RIGHT DOWN

In an effort to make the furniture as efficient as the structure itself, Rauser designed a sprawling built-in sofa with ample storage below the seat cushions.

WARMING UP

The home's energy-efficient design barely necessitates a wood-burning stove. Still, Rauser wanted one to stay true to the charm of a traditional farmhouse hearth. To give the small appliance more presence, it sits elevated atop a steel wood-storage box.

TUCKED IN

Stairwells are a drain on both time and budget. To make this home earn its keep, Rauser designed a modular shelving system along the base for books, keepsakes and even a flat-screen television. Further maximizing the efficiency, the laundry is stealthily housed under the stairs.

TOP SHELF
With no view to speak of on this side of the house, Rauser chose to forgo a traditional window over the kitchen sink in favor of streamlined open shelving, made from plywood scraps.

LIGHT POURS IN FROM A CONCEALED SKYLIGHT AND BOUNCES OFF THE STAINLESS STEEL CABINETRY AND GRANITE COUNTERTOPS.

FARMHOUSE FAVORITE
A WOOD-BURNING STOVE CREATES A COZY SPOT.

made for a 500-year life span—that's how tough it is." A happy by-product of the design? Exposed interior framing makes for a decidedly rough-hewn aesthetic. To keep costs low, the project brought hearty, humble materials—pipe fittings, subflooring and plywood, to name a few—front and center. The latter was used to craft the home's interior walls and also resulted in some serious debate. "We went back and forth on whether to leave the wood as is or paint it," explains Rauser. "We ultimately compromised with a solid body stain, which gave the calming white finish but was thin enough to let the wood's knots and imperfections shine through." The rustic, textured surfaces, which prove a perfect juxtaposition to the homeowner's sleek furnishings and collection of black-and-white photography, have a worn-in look that gives the impression the house has been there for years. One thing's for sure: It's not going anywhere any time soon. ∎

"

This house is made for a 500-year life span—that's how tough it is."

ERIC RAUSER

▶
MODERN EDGE
The bathroom vanity takes a cue from the office desk, with a plywood top and a base made of pipe fittings. The shower (below) gets a cheery jolt by way of a skylight that showcases the white subway tile.

PLYWOOD INSERTED BETWEEN THE FRAMEWORK CREATES INSTANT SHELVING.

▲
MAKING SPACE
At the top of the stairs, Rauser transformed potential throwaway space into a super-functional home office. The built-in desk was constructed from plywood and pipe fittings painted black for an industrial look.

FARMHOUSE FAVORITE
LOUVER DOORS (ONCE NEEDED TO INCREASE AIRFLOW) NOW ADD PRETTY LINES.

ROCK ON

Vintage wool blanket? Patinated leather chair? Kickin' guitar? Check! Check! And (sound) check! These handsome accents help what could have easily been a ho-hum bedroom strike a hip, handsome note. Also cool: the casement window, which swings open for pleasant second-story cross breezes.

*GRAPHIC
BLACK-AND-WHITE
PHOTOGRAPHY
ADDS MODERN
EDGE.*

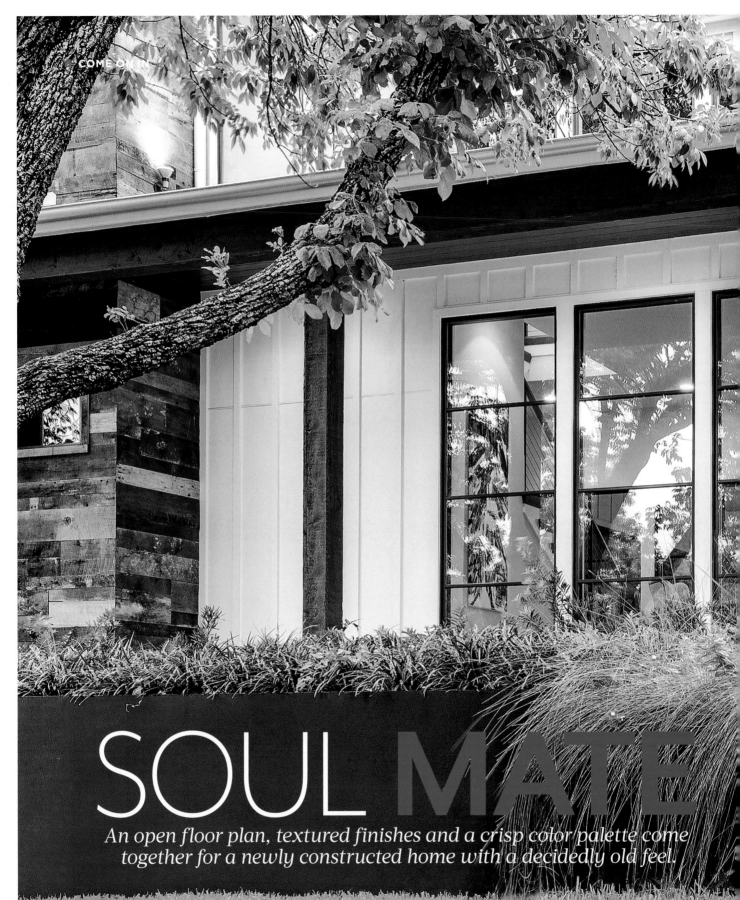

SOUL MATE

An open floor plan, textured finishes and a crisp color palette come together for a newly constructed home with a decidedly old feel.

102 MODERN FARMHOUSE MADE EASY

MIX UP
A range of materials (wood siding, textured brick) and architectural elements (varied roofline, different window shapes) give the impression the brand-new home has evolved and been added to over time.

❝

I wanted to add personality with accents like wood instead of fussy fabrics.”

STEPHANIE DAUWE

When your home is located in a woodsy stretch within the Dallas city limits, it's no exaggeration to say that only a farmhouse will do. As Rosewood Custom Builders set out to help a client construct a home in the Lakewood neighborhood, the team immediately knew what style they wanted for the young family—a modern take on a traditional farmhouse, with clean lines and plenty of large windows. "Lakewood is a little oasis in the middle of a lot of chaos. And it's a hub for outdoor activity. I wanted this house to have that same escape-from-it-all feel, as well as a strong connection to the outdoors," explains Stephanie Dauwe, the head designer on the project. "A fresh take on a farmhouse felt like the way to execute that."

That farmhouse interpretation was rooted in an open floor plan to maximize gathering and time together. "Part of the reason farmhouses are having a moment is their strong feeling of community and hospitality," says Stephanie. Rosewood also prioritized locally sourced materials. "Back in the day, farmhouses were built with what people had access to on the property. They didn't have the luxury of bringing things in from hundreds or thousands of miles away," explains Christopher Dauwe, Stephanie's brother, who oversees the company's construction operations. "We forged this house using organic materials that are substrates of the Earth. Almost everything is from a radius of 50 miles or less." For example, the beautifully rough-hewn wood that appears on various surfaces throughout

◀

FASHION STATEMENT
Designer Stephanie Dauwe often looks to clients' clothing choices as inspiration for the interiors. In the case of this project, the homeowners' favorite sports team meant they're often decked out in blue, black and white. She followed suit by infusing the trio of shades into almost every room.

FROST BITE

The wet bar's glass-fronted cabinets feature a frosty finish that adds subtle luminescence to the room. Below, the hexagon tiles add to the luster.

MIND THE GAP

The kitchen also features striking nickel gap paneling, which is a dead ringer for popular shiplap but more affordable to install. With this style, the boards do not overlap but instead are placed a "nickel's gap" apart from one another. The less complicated-woodwork results in a lower price tag.

FARMHOUSE FAVORITE
BRASS HARDWARE AND FIXTURES ARE A WAY TO ADD ABUNDANT WARMTH.

SHAKER-STYLE CABINETRY IS A CLASSIC, CLEAN-LINED LOOK.

HEAVY METAL
This informal dining space has some edge by way of hard-hitting details such as the spiky, aged-iron chandelier and iron-topped farmhouse table. Nailhead trim on the elegant wingbacks further galvanizes the look.

> 66
> Back in the day, farmhouses were built from materials on the property. We tried to do the same here."
>
> CHRISTOPHER DAUWE

WALK THIS WAY
Who says a hallway has to be an afterthought? With a few simple upgrades (a trio of brass mirrors, floor-to-ceiling windows), this one is elevated from pass-through to focal point, further building on the texture and material mix found in the home.

FARMHOUSE FAVORITE
FLOOR-TO-CEILING WINDOWS MAXIMIZE INDOOR/OUTDOOR STYLE.

STRAIGHT & NARROW

Minimalism rules in the dreamy master
retreat. Slim blue tiles and modern details,
like a floating vanity, walk a stylish line.

*DECONSTRUCTED
SCONCES INCORPORATE
AN INDUSTRIAL ELEMENT.*

**FARMHOUSE
FAVORITE**
*WHITE ROOMS
WITH A SINGLE
POP OF BLUE MAKE
FOR A TRANQUIL,
TIMELESS DESIGN.*

RUSTIC OASIS
The master bedroom's serene ambience is anchored by an overdyed blue Oushak rug. While the room is sophisticated, farmhouse embellishments, such as the reclaimed wood ceiling, help it feel connected to the rest of the house.

TALL, ELEGANT TABLE LAMPS EXAGGERATE THE HEIGHT OF A ROOM.

BLUE LAGOON
The shower's soothing but impactful blue tiles bring a reflecting-pool effect to the airy master bath.

the house was salvaged from a dilapidated barn just down the road. Similarly, they sourced the stone—found on the hearths—locally from Lueders, Texas.

With those thoughtful materials in play, Stephanie decided to let finishes do the heavy lifting, both in terms of form and function. "I wanted to add personality with hardscapes like the wood, rather than rely on fussy furniture and window treatments," she says. "I also wanted to avoid anything requiring too much upkeep. The entire house is no more than a room wide so it's in constant conversation (read muddy shoes!) with the outside."

What's more, these materials are subtly repeated rather than incorporated in over-the-top, look-at-me installations. "I find it much more interesting to use finishes in small doses rather than on every wall," explains Stephanie. "The result is a new house that feels as though it might have evolved over time." (In actuality, that evolution took a short and impressive 10 months from groundbreaking to move-in day!) Today, the happy new residents are living in a home as rich and textured as the view just beyond their windows. ∎

111

TAKE IT OUTSIDE
Just as the interiors feature many natural elements, the outdoor spaces include living room niceties such as plush chairs.

THE WHITE FACADE GIVES THE FIREPIT A MODERN PRESENCE.

SIT A SPELL
Billowy ferns? Ceiling fans?
Rocking chairs? Holly's
128-year-old cottage
has all the hallmarks of a
sit-a-spell front porch. Plus,
the ultimate farmhouse
accessory—a good dog
waiting by the front door.

FARMHOUSE FAVORITE
ROCKING CHAIRS ADD WELCOMING CURB APPEAL.

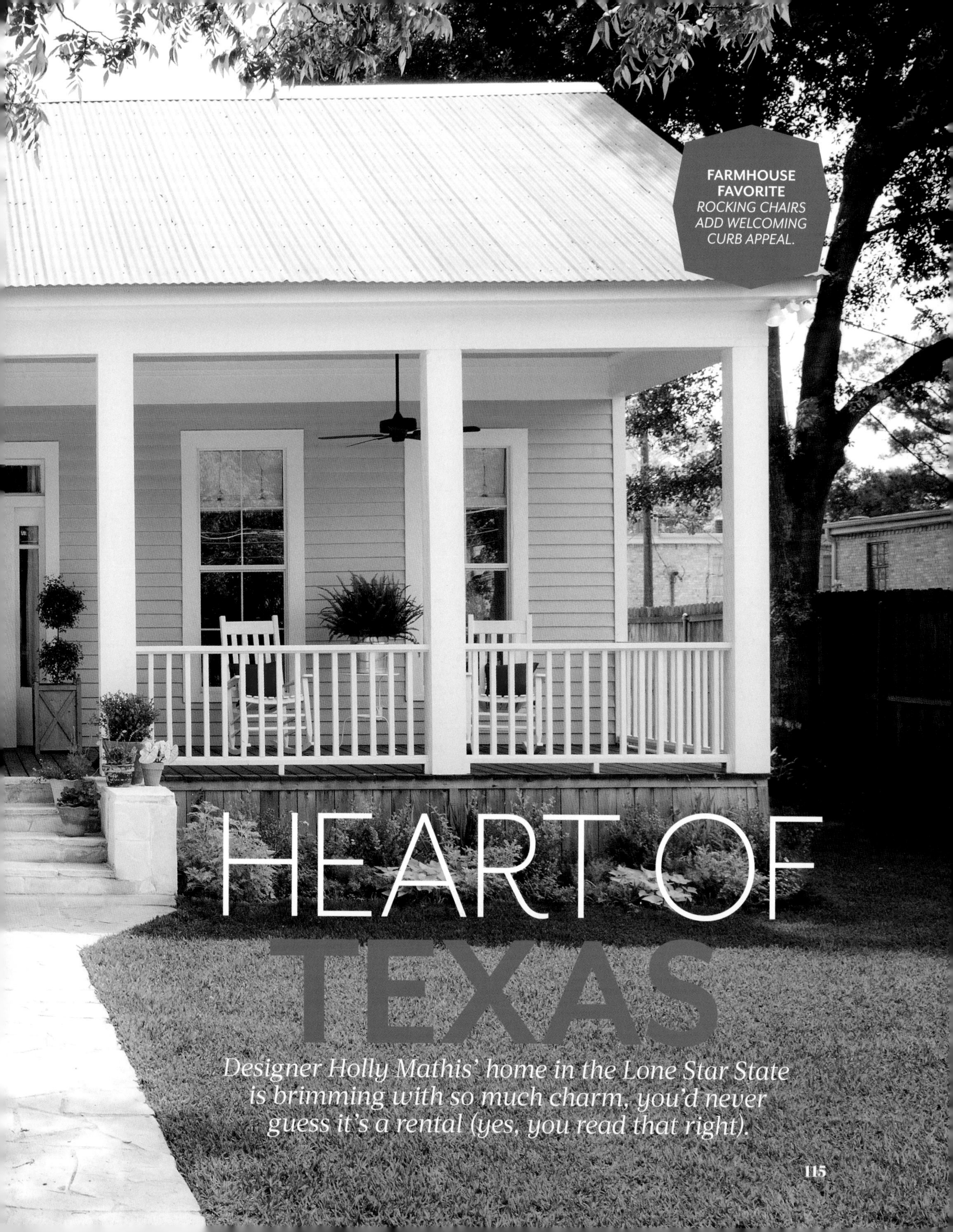

HEART OF TEXAS

Designer Holly Mathis' home in the Lone Star State is brimming with so much charm, you'd never guess it's a rental (yes, you read that right).

FEATHERED NEST

Holly's most prized item in the house (besides dog Hunter, that is) just happens to be the living room's blue heron portrait. The archival Audubon print features Holly's favorite bird and was created by her dear friend Melisse Campbell of Campbell's Melange in New Orleans (campbellsmelange.com).

WINDOWS GO SANS CURTAINS FOR A SUNNY, LESS-FUSSY LOOK.

BUCK UP

Holly collects German roe deer antlers by the dozens. Here, they make for a cool, chic display between windows.

▶ TUCKED IN

A narrow dining room chair proves just the right size for an airy reading alcove.

PERFECT PAIRING

New (acrylic tray; starburst accent) and old (antique portrait; framed ledger from an old Texas business) come together for a curated vignette on a marble-topped credenza.

"No way." That was Holly Mathis' response when her mother said she'd found the perfect rental home for Holly and her two sons to make a fresh start. "It was a newly renovated, historic home. I figured it couldn't possibly be within my budget," she explains. To appease her mom, she went to take a look. Holly discovered, much to her surprise, that not only could she swing the rent, but the home was located a mere two blocks from the boys' school. "It just seemed meant to be," says Holly. "The moment I walked in, I felt like I'd been sent a soft place to land." And there was more to that sense of belonging than the practical aspects of

FARMHOUSE FAVORITE
OLD PHOTOS BRING A RESIDENT'S FAMILY HISTORY FRONT AND CENTER.

TEAM WORK
An old church pew and a series of yard-long photos (long, skinny team photos that were popular in the early 19th century) transform a narrow hallway into a pretty-as-a-picture spot to kick off your boots.

FIRST IMPRESSIONS
Faded, pressed botanicals and a distressed gold mirror set an elegant, but relaxed, tone the minute you step in the front door.

location and price. With 11-foot ceilings, sunny rooms and original pine floors, the circa-1890 cottage spoke to her designer heart.

Rental agreement in hand, Holly set out to create a home reflective of her inviting farmhouse style. The first task? Warming up the cool gray walls. "It wouldn't have been my choice of paint color, but it's a rental so what can you do?" says Holly. To remedy, she layered in pretty patterns, jute rugs and plenty of linen textiles. Next, she looked to a smart mix of catalog buys and antiques to infuse the home

with style and substance. "I love vintage pieces, but I like to mix those with newer finds so rooms feel fresh and not too cluttered," she explains. Take the beautifully weathered dining table. "It has impossibly deep cracks that I just love," says Holly. It's paired with reproduction French dining chairs. ("They were a gift from my mom. We do furniture instead of jewelry!" she adds.) Together, the table and chairs form a happy marriage of old and new.

While there are plenty of big-box buys balancing out the chippy finds, Holly admits that it's the latter that steal the

119

CLASSIC VIBE
Buffalo check café curtains
and an iron drying rack make
the newly refurbished space
feel as though it's looked
this way for generations.

*BURNISHED SILVER
KEEPS THE CHINA
COLLECTION FROM
FEELING TWEE.*

AN OLD LINEN CABINET PROVIDES ADDITIONAL STORAGE.

CREATIVE CONSTRUCTION
When she first moved in, the country kitchen didn't have an island. Scrappy Holly crafted one by wrapping two lower kitchen cabinets (purchased from a local liquidator) in V-groove paneling and topping them with a butcher-block countertop.

there are far, far better things ahead than any we leave behind.
C.S. Lewis

"
I love vintage pieces, but I like to mix them in with newer finds for a fresh feel."

HOLLY MATHIS

COLD MEATS · VEGETABLES & FRUIT

CROWN MOLDING GIVES A SMART FINISH TO THE STOCK CABINETS.

OLD-FASHIONED CHARM
The antique grocery sign brings a bit of rustic beauty to the clean-lined white kitchen. The butcher-block island top echoes the space's warm tones.

FARMHOUSE FAVORITE *OPEN SHELVES TURN EVERYDAY ITEMS INTO WORKS OF ART.*

PITCHING IN
Pouring on the charm in the kitchen: Holly's collection of ironstone pitchers displayed on the open shelving. (She picks up a new piece each year at the nearby Round Top Antiques Fair.)

show. In the simple kitchen, for example, you'll find white subway tile from Lowe's and butcher-block countertops from Ikea. But the space shines thanks to the perfectly patinated old grocery sign that measures just over 9 feet long; Holly purchased it, somewhat fittingly, at Leftovers Antiques (leftoversantiques.com), one of her favorite local shops.

Holly was able to make some impactful design changes, including swapping out ho-hum light fixtures for eye-catching ones. But at the end of the day she had to remain cognizant of the rental status. "I'm a draperies girl," says Holly. "I always push my clients toward them. But with tall ceilings, it would have cost a fortune to do panels everywhere. That just didn't make sense in a rental."

OPTICAL ILLUSION
In Holly's bedroom (the one spot where she splurged on curtains!) is an extra-wide, full-length mirror that helps the space feel bigger by reflecting natural light. A ghost chair (right) wrapped in a dainty slipcover adds to the gleaming look.

Room by room, Holly layered in her seamless mix of pretty and practical until each space in the airy abode was beaming with storied style. "Yes, this is a rental house, but it's also one of the loveliest places I've ever lived. It truly feels like home," Holly says. Turns out, mother does know best. ∎

▶
ON DISPLAY
Boyhood treasures such as flags, globes, trophies and a stately deer head make for a kid's bedroom vignette that will easily transition to the teen years.

A HANDSOME GALLERY WALL SPIFFS UP A BIG-BOX STORE DRESSER.

FARMHOUSE FAVORITE
FLAGS—BOTH OLD AND NEW—PUT A PRIDE OF PLACE ON FULL DISPLAY.

BOOK IT
While Holly avoids slapping paint on true antiques, less-precious furniture is fair game. Take the bookcase in her son's room: She's had it since college and it's on its "hundredth" coat. For a clean look, she uses a paint slightly lighter or darker than the surrounding wall color.

FARMHOUSE FAVORITE
TRANSOM WINDOWS RECALL A BYGONE ERA WHEN THEY WERE NEEDED FOR CROSS BREEZES.

INTO THE BLUE
The informal family room, located just off the kitchen, is anchored by a pair of sofas upholstered in a fabric that can take a beating. The choppy green coffee table adds an equally durable pop of color to the room.

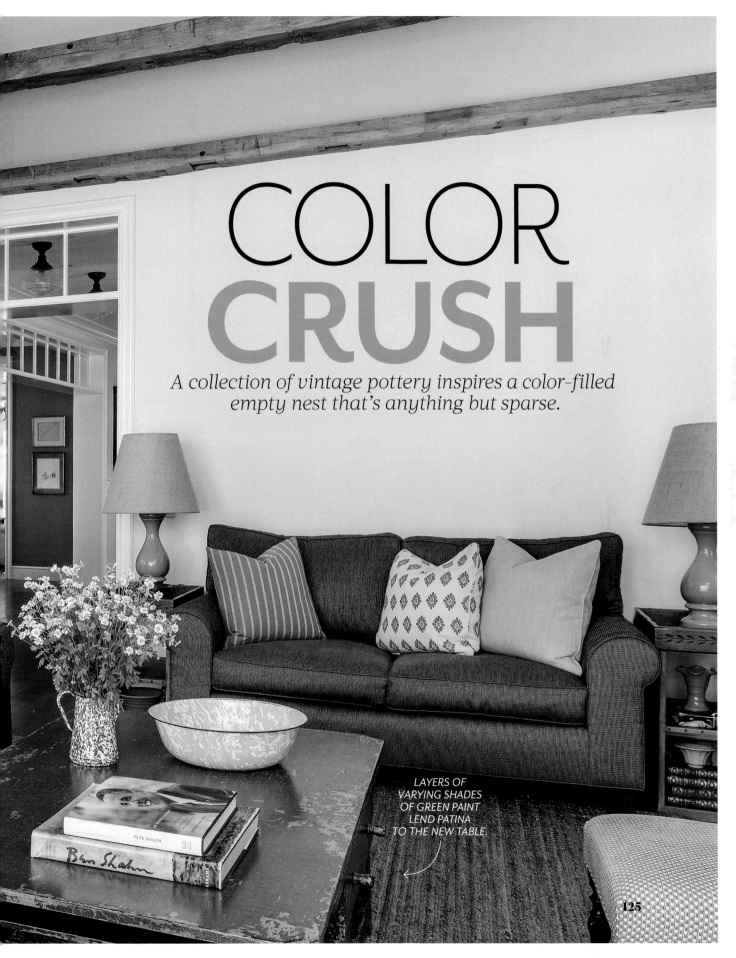

COLOR
CRUSH

A collection of vintage pottery inspires a color-filled empty nest that's anything but sparse.

LAYERS OF
VARYING SHADES
OF GREEN PAINT
LEND PATINA
TO THE NEW TABLE.

NAILHEAD TRIM BRINGS A TAILORED VIBE TO THIS ARMCHAIR.

It started with pottery. Bauer Pottery, to be specific. The made-in-California line debuted shortly after the Great Depression and has been making waves ever since, thanks to its splashy hues. A collector for nearly 30 years, homeowner Carole first took note of designer Alison Kandler's work when she noticed her beloved dishware prominently featured in one of the designer's previous projects. At the time, Carole was about to embark on a much-pined-for renovation of the house she and her husband, Doug, had called home since the 1980s. Smitten with Kandler's style, she reached out to her to oversee the project, which took a behind-the-times Spanish colonial to an of-the-moment farmhouse. "The couple had raised four children there and had been dreaming about updating it for a long time," Kandler recalls. "Her kids begged her not to change a thing but she was ready!"

Naturally, Bauer Pottery, which Kandler also collects, became square one for the design inspiration. "She probably has the biggest collection I've ever seen—and that's really saying something," admits Kandler. "The pottery's bright color scheme was an easy fit for her aesthetic and a laid-back farmhouse style." And so

◀

WELL-READ

Cozy! That was the name of the game in the library. There, the walls are lined with a nubby grass cloth, built-in bookcases are backed with (surprise!) orange wallpaper, and an impossibly plush armchair provides a spot to curl up with a book.

▼

WONDER WALLS

The dining room, visible from virtually every room downstairs, commands attention with a shimmering orange grass cloth wall covering. The room is also home to an inset hutch custom designed to showcase more than 50 pieces of Bauer Pottery.

◀

CZECH IT OUT

The homeowner's smaller collection of Czech floral pottery complements the home's Bauer-inspired color scheme, as do the vintage books arranged by hues.

▼

ENTRY LEVEL

Just inside the front door, a wonderfully weathered oak table and a basket full of Bauer Pottery give the home country charm from the get-go.

LARGE PLANTERS ADD STORAGE BELOW.

inky blues, vibrant turquoises, buttery yellows, rusty reds and sprightly oranges proved central to the house's palette. Emphasis on the orange: "It's just her color," says Kandler. "Some people are anti-orange but it makes her very, very happy. So I, of course, used it every chance I got." From interior doors to throw pillows, she infused nearly every space with Carole's signature hue. The color takes an especially central role in the dining room, where the walls are covered with vivacious orange grass cloth. "You see the dining room as soon as you walk through the front door so it really sets the tone," adds Kandler.

When it came to furnishings, she and Carole also had a connection. The hutch that had long housed Carole's collection of Bauer ware had been crafted by the designer's favorite furniture maker, Mulligan's Furniture. Building off that design, they enlisted Mulligan's to make multiple new pieces for the home, including the dining room table, family room coffee table and guest bed. While the pieces are new, they have an authentic feel. The items were created with layers of different shades of paint and then

IN THE ROUND
The sunny breakfast nook is home to a round dining table that Kandler chose both for its classic country curves and pretty patina.

FARMHOUSE FAVORITE
TIE-BACK SEAT CUSHIONS ARE AN OLD-FASHIONED TOUCH.

129

COOL & COLLECTED

Kandler kept the kitchen intentionally neutral to better showcase the homeowner's prized pottery. Rush-back barstools and wooden shelves with iron brackets give the new kitchen old style.

EXTENDING THE
BUILT-IN SHELVING
TO THE CROWN
MOLDING DRAWS
THE EYE UP.

SCREEN TIME
An old screen door,
painted a vibrant teal,
brings a fun, undeniably
farmhouse element to the
kitchen. The open design
also gives a peek at the
pretty staples inside.

> "After raising four kids here, the homeowners were ready to update. They'd been dreaming about it for a long time."
> ALISON KANDLER

FLOWER BED
In the master bedroom, orange gives way to rosy red, which appears as the anchor color in a number of floral motifs. Beyond, striped grass cloth wallpaper creates a fresh take on classic wainscoting.

ANTIQUE WICKER ADDS A RELAXED, PORCH-LIKE FEEL.

FARMHOUSE FAVORITE
SPOOL BEDS, BOTH OLD AND NEW, SHOWCASE AMERICAN CRAFTSMANSHIP AT ITS FINEST.

slightly distressed, creating an evolved-over-time effect. "This furniture is sturdy and comfortable and that's a very farmhouse trait," says Kandler.

With the project now complete, the happy, inviting ome has become the main gathering spot for holiday get-togethers and family celebrations of all sort. And, yes, the once-reluctant grown children are frequent guests at the "empty nest." But as Kandler sees it, this home's best days are still to come. "There are no grandchildren yet, but we have planned for them," she explains. "There are reading nooks and plenty of spots to pull out a board game," no matter what the future may bring. ∎

COOL IT
One way Kandler made the repeated use of orange work? Merely using it as an accent in some spaces. In the guest bedroom it's paired with an abundance of turquoise. The cool undertones temper the fiery hue.

The furniture here is sturdy and comfortable.
That's a very farmhouse trait!"

ALISON KANDLER

*COLORFUL
CERAMIC KNOBS
ADD INSTANT
WHIMSY.*

**TAKE THE
FLOOR**
With its myriad of
wallpaper, walls steal
the show in most of
the home's spaces.
In this bathroom,
however, Kandler
flipped the script with
vibrant turquoise
ceramic floor tiles.

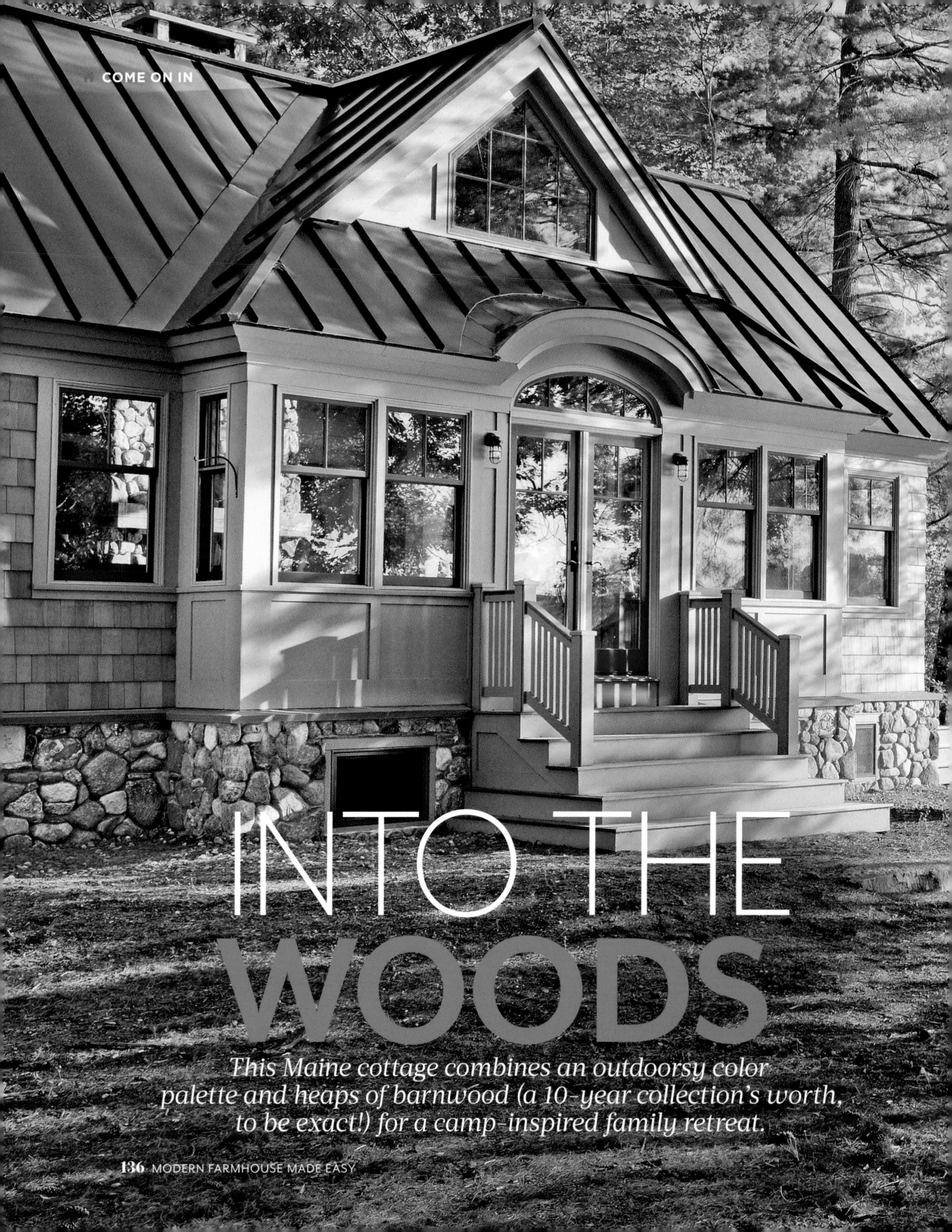

INTO THE WOODS

This Maine cottage combines an outdoorsy color palette and heaps of barnwood (a 10-year collection's worth, to be exact!) for a camp-inspired family retreat.

HIDE AND SEEK
The fieldstone foundation, cedar-shake siding and dark-brown aluminum roof were selected to make the house look tucked in among the trees.

137

WATER'S EDGE
A humble plank dock mimics the
cabin's nothing-to-excess approach.

> ❝
> ## It was important to me that this house felt like a camp lodge—but not in an overdone way, like weekend homes sometimes do."
>
> KRISTINA CRESTIN

ROOM WITH A VIEW
At the windowless end of the
dining room, Crestin created a
"view" with a landscape painting
that features saturated colors and
textured brushstrokes reminiscent
of paint-by-number artwork but
far larger than the retro staple.

When designer Kristina Crestin's clients told her the main idea for their remote Maine lake house was "a sleepaway camp, with no drywall anywhere," she had to pinch herself. "You rarely get a directive that presents so much opportunity for creativity and unexpected materials," she says. But that's just what the family wanted, and they looked to build a quaint cabin within the same 1,200-square-foot footprint as the house that had once stood on the property. (The original plan was to salvage the homestead, but it proved beyond repair.)

Not one to haphazardly install materials, Crestin carefully considered what would go where and was determined to avoid a single material in abundance, lest the overall look read too Lincoln Log. "Originally, we thought reclaimed barnwood on the walls but feared it would go dark—not to mention, it's a little rough to be the material you're closest to," Crestin recalls. Instead, she devised a formula of barnwood on the ceilings, oak V-groove paneling (stained, not painted, to let knotty imperfections shine through) on the walls and wide-plank maple floors with a hand-scraped finish.

Even with that economy of materials, the project still took *a lot* of wood. To find enough, Crestin shopped local,

SET IN STONE
Each piece of locally sourced fieldstone was hand-placed to give the towering stone fireplace a textured but not choppy look. A chunky raw-wood mantel complements the organic focal point.

139

UNDER-THE-EAVES WINDOWS KEEP THE BARNWOOD CEILINGS FROM GOING TOO DARK.

GREEN WITH ENVY

Stained cabinetry would have been the expected choice for the wood-drenched home. But Crestin broke the mold by swathing it in a yellow-green shade that gives the room a jolt of personality. Concrete countertops and unlacquered brass hardware, which requires little maintenance and will acquire a striking patina over time, ground the eclectic look.

FARMHOUSE FAVORITE
PAINTED CABINETRY MIMICS OLD CUPBOARDS.

A METAL BACKSPLASH ADDS INDUSTRIAL STYLE TO THE SPACE.

RAINBOW CONNECTION
The cabinetry color is matched with a range and hood in an equally vibrant shade of blue. Together, they make for an amped-up take on the colors just outside the window.

FARMHOUSE FAVORITE
EXPOSED BLACK PIPE FITTINGS STYLISHLY WALK THE LINE BETWEEN FARM AND FACTORY.

NO
BODY
LIKES
A

SMART

PERFECT PAIRINGS

Rustic and industrial, old and new come together in this smart bedroom, which comfortably sleeps three. A wood-paneled bunk features guardrails crafted from black pipe fittings, while an antique bobbin chair plays nice with a monochromatic, modern take on taxidermy.

◀

ON A ROLL

When Crestin discovered the barn door's wonderfully distressed rusty-red paint job had accidentally been stripped by the crew, she went with plan B—a medium-tone stain that's equally as inviting.

▼

MELLOW YELLOW

After yellow-green tile was installed in the shower, Crestin felt the only thing to do was envelop the entire bathroom in the hue. She then color-matched paint to coat the V-groove paneling. "It helps the small space read as more cohesive and expansive," she explains. Rounding out the kid-friendly space is a rubber gnome stool, spray-painted a fittingly cheerful shade of bright blue.

so to speak, enlisting area carpenter Ron Dunn, who found a mother lode of barnwood in a nearby field. "This person had been collecting it for a decade," Crestin recalls. "Ron rolled up and said, 'We'll take it all!'"

Crestin also looked outside to inspire the home's palette of blues and greens. "You can honor what you see out the window, but it doesn't have to be a strict execution. Dial it up a notch!" she says. And that's just what she did, pushing the boundaries of the sky's and forest's hues with bold interpretations, including aqua and chartreuse.

Ultimately, both the interior and exterior work together to bring the outdoors in for a home that's "camp"—in the very best sense of the word. ∎

SHIPSHAPE

The bunk room features an ingenious layout with eight (yes, eight!) beds (four full, four twin) and an abundance of storage—including discreet drawers in the stair risers.

FARMHOUSE FAVORITE
THE BUNK ROOM NODS TO A FARMHOUSE'S SLEEP-A-CROWD ROOTS.

VINTAGE POSTERS ARE A NATURAL STARTING POINT FOR A CLASSIC COLOR PALETTE.

WE BELONG

✚

100% STRONG

1920

AID AND ABET

The house's notes of blue take an all-American turn in the bunk room, where the colors were inspired by old Red Cross posters.

FARMHOUSE FAVORITE
WOOD DECKING GIVES THE SWIMMING POOL A DOWN-HOME BORDER.

AN OLD FRUIT CRATE CAN STAND IN AS A SIDE TABLE.

MAKING A SPLASH
The saltwater pool has swimming hole appeal, thanks to an azure hue and a natural surrounding that gives the impression it's actually a spring-fed pond.

CALIFORNIA
DREAMING
A former wreck of a house gets turned sunny-side up.

L
ocation, location, location! In the beginning, that was all that could be said for the Newport Beach house designer Raili Clasen calls home. "Nothing drew me to the house. It was horrible," she recalls. "But I am a freak about natural light, and it had plenty of that. Better still, we had good friends living up and down the block." It was also centrally located for the beach—a serious perk for her surf-obsessed husband, Ryan, and their two sons. To take the house from "horrible" to something far more how-about-that, Clasen teamed up with area architect Eric Olsen to create a California take on the farmhouse aesthetic that also expanded upon the home's strong points of amazing light and a pretty lot.

▲ BLACK MAGIC
The near-black exterior puts a modern spin on the boxy design. Reclaimed-wood shutters set the tone for the many rustic details found within.

▶ TREAD LIGHTLY
A cozy living area connects the kitchen and dining room. Here, Clasen opted for soft pieces (slipcovered sofas, a camp chair, a cot turned coffee table) to contrast the hardscapes of the adjoining areas.

FARMHOUSE FAVORITE
AN EXPANSE OF BARNWOOD WILL "COUNTRY UP" THE MOST MOD OF SPACES.

BUZZ WORTHY

Key accents keep the coffee shop–inspired kitchen from feeling too, well, commercial. Case in point: the wood-wrapped range vent, the antique metal "American" sign and Clasen's own prized collection of vintage lunchboxes.

FARMHOUSE FAVORITE
BEEFY MARBLE COUNTERTOPS CAN HANDLE HIGH TRAFFIC.

AMERICA

THRIFT-SHOP PAINTINGS LOOK SHARP WHEN DISPLAYED IN A GROUP.

LOGGING IN
The home's head-turning art installation was actually a matter of budget. Clasen conceived the floor-to-ceiling "column" of logs when a stone fireplace of the same height (the ceilings measure a whopping 12 foot high) proved too costly. The woodsy focal point is complemented by an equally expansive raw-wood dining table.

First, they opened up the disjointed living spaces to create a central great room. "An open floor plan is something I'm always drawn to as a designer. But as a mom, it was a must," she explains. Starting from scratch also presented the opportunity for Clasen's creativity to run wild. Enter unexpected details such as hardwood floors laid on the diagonal (an idea she got from Anthropologie stores); a budget-friendly focal point of floor-to-ceiling logs; and quirky accents, like a bike rack right alongside the formal dining table.

The room with the most design moxie may be the kitchen. She modeled it after a commercial cook space, with dark-paneled walls; flat-front, locker-style cabinetry; and an island that incorporates both marble and butcher-block tops. "I wanted it to feel like you'd stepped inside a cool coffee shop, not just another kitchen," she explains.

BOCCE RULE
1. Hold drink in non throwing hand
2. Form 2 teams of 2-4 players
3. One team throws pallino down c
   that player throws first bocce
4. Teams alternate tossing bocce
   trying to get closest to pallino o
   knock the opponents balls away
5. The closest team scores points
   ball closer than opposing team
   An "official" instrument may be
   to measure

FIRST TEAM
WINS

▲

HOLDING COURT
Proving she's always up for fun, Clasen
transformed a side yard into a bocce court.
Along the fence is a chalkboard with the
family's cheeky rules of the game, including
"hold drink in nonthrowing hand."

▶

VINE AND DINE
A pergola crafted from cedar and blanketed
in trumpet vine (a plant known for its quick
growth and hummingbird-attracting blooms)
frames an alfresco-ready dining space.

The home's three bedrooms were adequate in size,
but the bathrooms were another story. Clasen and Olsen
revamped the washrooms to have more functionality and
personality. (Don't miss the boys' bathroom door!) While
the home skews modern, she didn't want to water down
the original farmhouse inspiration. Enter repeated uses of
barnwood, including the range hood in the kitchen and
the headboard in the master bedroom. ("We ordered a
pallet's worth and then used it in as many places as we
could before it ran out," she recalls.) There were also
fresh takes on country-home staples, such as barn doors
with a hip ocean mural and "wood" paneled walls that
are, in fact, wallpaper. She paired those country touches

with coastal accents, including an actual surfboard in the
master bedroom, to ensure the home felt, well, at home
in the area.

With friends up and down the street, Clasen also
invested time and attention into the outdoor living spaces,
including a bocce-ball court, a vine-encased pergola and
a pool. "This is California—the weather affords us the
opportunity to spend a lot of time outdoors," she says
of her decision to prioritize these areas when mapping
out her budget.

With the project complete, Clasen can safely say that the
earlier horror of a home is a distant memory—and the new
incarnation is a perfect (hang) ten. ■

KNOW *fun.*

FARMHOUSE FAVORITE
ANTLER ACCENTS, LIKE THIS OUTDOOR CHANDELIER, ENSURE THAT A SPACE IS ON POINT.

"
We ordered a pallet's worth of barnwood
and then used it in as many places
as we could before it ran out."

RAILI CLASEN

FARMHOUSE FAVORITE
ROPE LIGHTS ADD TEXTURE AND SAVE ON FLOOR SPACE.

DOOR PRIZE

When Clasen came across an old "Men's Washroom" door (yes, that's the original glass and lettering), nothing else would do for her sons' shared bathroom. That conviction wasn't without its tests; the door had to be reconfigured several times to fit the space. "Not my most budget-conscious design choice," recalls Clasen. "But totally worth it."

SUITE DIGS

Homeowners often opt for neutral and hotel-like ambiance in their master suite. Not Clasen! Instead, she poured on the personality, with an ocean-inspired escape that features unconventional details like two-tone walls and an honest-to-goodness surfboard. Unexpected texture packs a punch in the master bathroom. Here, a brick backsplash and concrete countertops take the place of more expected subway tile and marble.

LOCK STAR

Adding to the bathroom's all-boy vibe is a bank of lockers that were ordered from an online school-supply wholesaler and powder-coated blue for a rust-resistant finish.

155

BEGINNER'S
PLUCK

A repeat renovator shares her very first labor of love.

ALL IN THE FAMILY
Homeowner Holly Williams, daughter and granddaughter of Hank Williams Jr. and Sr., strikes a chord with her husband, Chris Coleman.

TIME TO CHILL
One of Williams' first antique
purchases—an expansive clock
she scored at a Paris flea market—
anchors the living room with
laid-back patina.

FARMHOUSE FAVORITE
MIXING MATERIALS LIKE BRICK, MARBLE, TILE AND WOOD GIVES A ROOM AMPLE WARMTH.

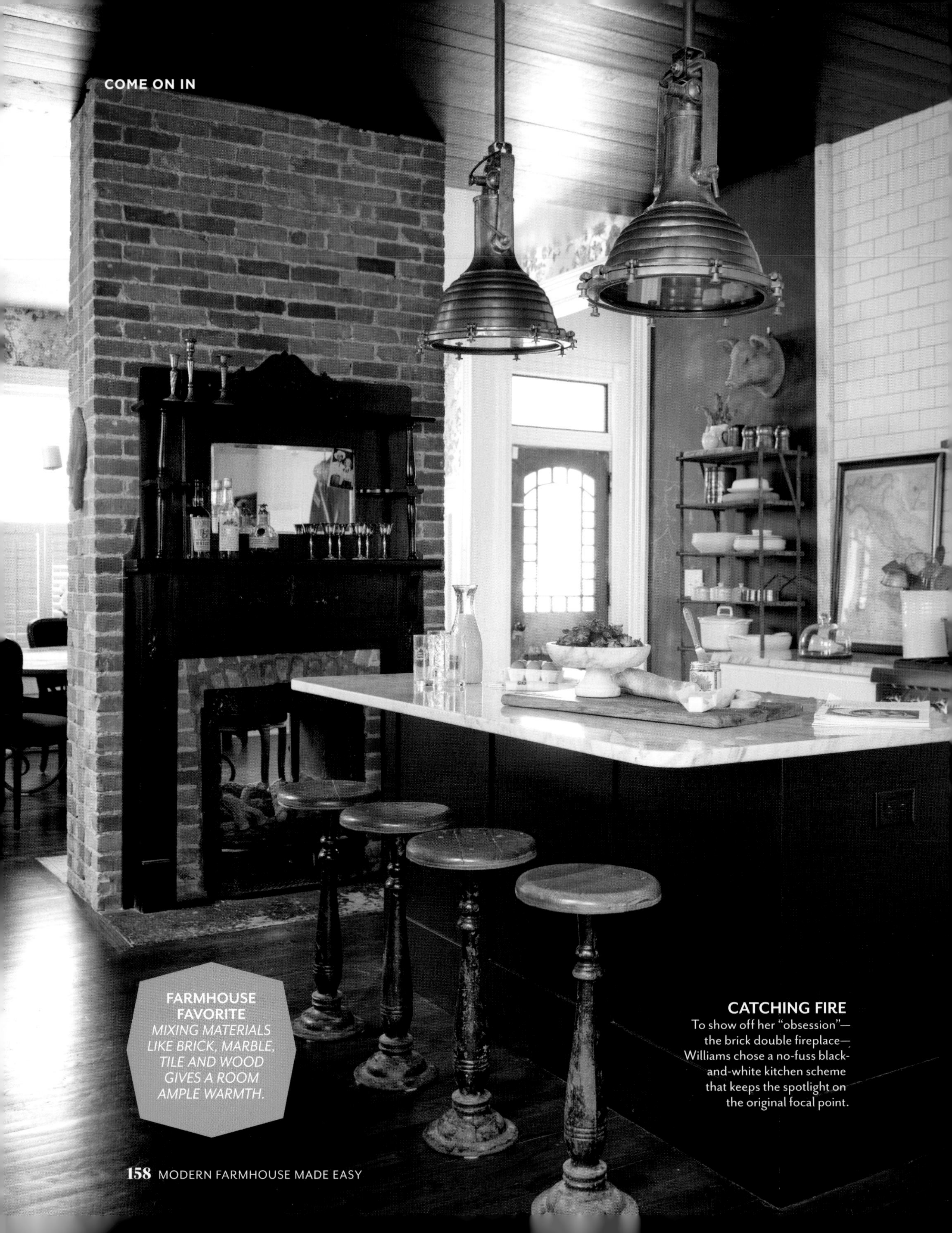

CATCHING FIRE
To show off her “obsession”—the brick double fireplace—Williams chose a no-fuss black-and-white kitchen scheme that keeps the spotlight on the original focal point.

PICTURE PERFECT
Inspired by a display in her grandmother's home, Williams transformed her entryway into a veritable art gallery brimming with family photos.

BACK IN BLACK
Williams used a striking shade of black paint to enliven tired paneling throughout the home.

Holly Williams knows a thing or two about giving an old house new life. The singer-songwriter and shop owner (she helms H. Audrey fashion boutique and six locations of the home-goods store White's Mercantile) has rehabbed a whopping nine homes over the past decade. While she's put her "blood, sweat and tears" into every single one, if pressed to play favorites, she'll admit to having a soft spot for her very first project. "I had no idea what I was doing when I took on that house. But it was all so much fun and I learned more than I could have ever imagined. It's hard to not be nostalgic for it," explains Williams. At the time she and her husband, Chris Coleman, an artist and fellow singer-songwriter, were looking to trade their downtown Nashville, Tennessee, loft for a home better suited to raising a family.

After looking high and low throughout Music City, they finally said "sold!" to a circa-1920s Sears Catalog bungalow

FARMHOUSE FAVORITE
WHETHER NEUTRAL OR BRIGHT, FLORAL WALLPAPERS PROVIDE A DOSE OF THE COUNTRYSIDE.

GATHER ROUND
While the metallic wallpaper adds undeniable glitz, Williams wanted to keep the dining room casual and inviting with a round antique table atop bare floors.

FAMILY PHOTOS EVOKE A SENSE OF THE PAST.

DRINK UP
Painted inky black, the kitchen mantel doubles as a serve-yourself bar. Unframed photos and artwork give it a homey look.

FARMHOUSE FAVORITE
VAULTED CEILINGS MAXIMIZE SPACE AND GIVE ROOMS AN AIRY ATMOSPHERE.

HELLO SUNSHINE

SLEEP ON IT
Williams made a last-minute renovation decision to take the ceiling to the eaves in the guest bedroom. Painted paneling draws attention to the feature.

in the then-emerging 12 South neighborhood. "It is no
exaggeration that I fell madly in love," explains Williams. "It
had 12-foot ceilings and some stunning original architecture
like the double fireplace separating the kitchen and dining
room." That is not to say the house wasn't without flaws.
Having previously been inhabited by 14 renters, it was
neglected and in near disrepair. An undaunted first-time
renovator, Williams jumped headfirst into the project,
not only bringing the home back from the brink, but also
adding a master suite and—get ready for this—an entire
second floor. She then adopted a hip palette of black and
white that felt safe for the rookie. "I've since learned to
embrace more color," she recalls. "But at the time, it felt
utterly daring to paint something gray!" ∎

◀

ROMANCE NOVEL
The master bedroom swaps gritty for sweet
with a frilly chandelier and canopy bed.

163

NEUTRAL
TERRITORY

*A subdued color palette allows texture to shine
at a family's forever home.*

ROCK AND ROLL

Anchoring the spacious living
room is an old cart turned
coffee table with handsomely
weathered wood. The antique
adds soul to a room full of new
furnishings, without calling too
much attention to itself.

GLASS-FRONT
CABINETS HELP
THE ROOM TO
APPEAR EVEN
MORE OPEN.

Sometimes what you're looking for is right in your own backyard. That idea rings true for Wendi and Jason Kliewer. When the couple, who are parents to two young children, were looking for a spot to put down roots, they were prepared to cast a very wide net. To their surprise, they found a flat, stunning lot a mere five streets over from their current home in Newport Beach, California. "We love this neighborhood and couldn't believe our good luck," Wendi recalls.

The property called for a new build, which meant the Kliewers could finally indulge an aesthetic they'd been eyeing for quite some time—modern farmhouses, particularly like those in California's Napa Valley. "We've spent a lot of time in that part of the state and fell for the combination of rustic and sophisticated,"

BOARD GAMES

Reclaimed wood left over from
the home's ceilings was used
to finish out a bookshelf nook,
bringing rustic charm to the
inconspicuous spot.

LET THERE BE LIGHT

Lighting is critical with a neutral
color palette. Enter pieces like
this duo of arched table lamps,
which cast a cozy glow over
the low-slung linen sofa.

LOOKING UP
Wendi knew she wanted to incorporate reclaimed wood in the home. But where? She settled on the ceiling as a spot that would make a statement without overpowering.

FARMHOUSE FAVORITE
WIRE CABLE STAIR RAILINGS RISE TO THE OCCASION WITH HIP INDUSTRIAL STYLE.

*KNOTTY
IMPERFECTIONS
ADD EARTHY BEAUTY
TO A ROOM.*

BARE NECESSITIES
In an effort to keep things casual
and show off those stunning floors,
Wendi skipped a dining room rug in
favor of striking bare floors.

169

CABINET-FRONTED
APPLIANCES CREATE
A COHESIVE LOOK.

says Wendi. To achieve the look, they teamed up with architect Eric Olsen, who helped the family realize their vision with a symmetric floor plan that capitalized on all that California sunshine. Reclaimed wood became a central design element, with Wendi strategically planning the placement of each board. To keep the focus on that rough-hewn craftsmanship, she also embraced a whole-house palette of creams and grays that complemented, rather than competed, with the wood tones. The result is the forever farmhouse for which the family had been pining. As Wendi explains: "This house is just around the corner from the old one, but it truly feels worlds away." ◼

◀

DYNAMIC DUO
The kitchen's sophisticated design was all about mixing materials in one of two shades: gray (cabinetry, hardware and range hood) and white (tile, ceiling and countertops).

FARMHOUSE FAVORITE
A STATEMENT RANGE HOOD TURNS AN ACCENT MATERIAL INTO A SUPERSTAR PLAYER.

FARMHOUSE FAVORITE
WHITE SUBWAY TILES EASILY MIX BYGONE CHARM AND CLEAN, MODERN LINES.

ROOTED IN STYLE

The one vibrant spot of color in the achromatic kitchen? A bounty of succulents. The rich greens, and a few purples for good measure, pop against the neutral backdrop.

A SHEET METAL PENDANT BEAUTIFULLY REFLECTS THE NATURAL LIGHT.

SANDS OF TIME
Wendi planned to refinish the once-dark breakfast table (just the right size for the compact space). Surprise! When she sanded it down she found the perfect pale shade—no staining required.

*GRAY PAINT
COMPLEMENTS
WEATHERED
WOOD TONES.*

BRICKLAYERS ARMS
BROCKLEY CROSS
BROCKLEY RISE
CATFORD GARAGE
CATFORD RUSHEY GREEN
DOWNHAM WAY BROMLEY ROAD
ELEPHANT & CASTLE
FARRINGDON STREET
GROVE PARK
HOXTON BARING STREET
MANOR HOUSE STATION
MOORGATE FINSBURY SQUARE
NEW CROSS GARAGE
NEWINGTON GREEN
TURNPIKE LANE STN

ROLL CALL
The gallery at the top of
the stairs features one of
Wendi's favorite antique
finds: a London bus roll
that once announced
arrivals and departures
across the pond.

FARMHOUSE FAVORITE *FOUR-POSTER BEDS ADD DRAMA AND SHOW OFF OLD-FASHIONED CRAFTSMANSHIP.*

BRUSH WITH GREATNESS
Wendi went through dozens of paints to find the perfect not-too-dark shade of gray for the master bedroom. The winner? Repose Gray by Sherwin-Williams.

TOTALLY FLOORED
There are no wood tones in the master bathroom, but the lovely gray veining in the herringbone-pattern marble floor echoes the home's organic feel.

175

*CERAMIC SPHERES
ARE A SCULPTURAL
ADDITION TO A
FIREPLACE.*

❝

This house is refined but also
completely relaxed. There's a balance
here that just makes us feel at home."

WENDI KLIEWER

FARMHOUSE FAVORITE
NOTHING SAYS COUNTRY LIFE (EVEN IN CALIFORNIA!) LIKE A SWEET ROPE SWING.

▲
BORDERLINE
Much of the property was cleared to make way for the new home; however, the Kliewers kept as many trees as they could along the property line, including this towering oak.

◄
VIEWFINDER
The Kliewers invested a lot of time (and dirt!) to create a perfectly flat backyard, allowing the deck to align with the front door to create a striking view from the moment you step inside.

PEAK FORM
Designer and homeowner Sherry McKuin oriented the home's two-story windows in a north-facing direction to maximize the views of the Topatopa Mountains.

MATERIAL
WORLD

Cedar? Concrete? Stone? Check, check and check! This mountain escape boasts resilient finishes befitting its rough-hewn locale.

792 (1)   Picturesque

4C4-2   Picturesque

If your home overlooks one of the country's most scenic mountain ranges, it's no exaggeration to say that only a farmhouse will do. And so, when Sherry McKuin set out to build a home for her family in Ojai, California, at the foot of the Topatopa Mountains, she immediately knew what style it should be—a modern take on the farmhouse aesthetic, with clean lines and plenty of large windows. (These are views of the Los Padres National Forest we're talking about.) She was also dead set on letting the finishes do the talking, in terms of both form and function. "I wanted to add personality with hardscapes, like tile and reclaimed wood, rather than put too much focus on statement-making furniture and window treatments," explains

▼

GAME PLAN
"The architecture of the house was inspired by the idea of a very minimal form, almost like a Monopoly piece," explains McKuin. The simple design was clad in glass, cedar and stone to meld with the property.

FARMHOUSE FAVORITE
A TWO-SIDED HEARTH MAXIMIZES SPACE FOR FIRESIDE CHATS AND S'MORE ROASTS.

SHOP LOCAL
"The house just naturally took on the colors
and textures of Ojai," explains McKuin, who
purchased much of the home's furniture and
virtually all the artwork in the neighboring town
of Ojai, an enclave of artisans and makers.

181

My main goal was that the house not be
fussy in any way. The kids can run through,
friends can spill wine—not a problem."

SHERRY McKUIN

SPLIT DECISION
The large kitchen afforded McKuin
the opportunity to use a variety of
materials. Most notable: Carrara
marble on the wall-hugging
counters and soapstone atop the
expansive island.

183

TILE FILES
That's no porcelain tile! For an understated material among the other natural elements, McKuin opted for a backsplash crafted from wood tile with a geometric design.

McKuin. "I avoided anything requiring much upkeep. This is a house in the mountains—the last thing it should be is precious."

To put her "finishes-over-flourishes" vision into action, she enlisted a wide range of materials to give the home depth and character. She started on the exterior of the home, with cedar planks that artfully blend with the topography. Indoors, surfaces such as concrete, Silestone, unlacquered brass and brick were incorporated for clean-lined surfaces with serious durability. While floor-to-ceiling windows (aluminum offerings that are a dead ringer for steel!) do most of the work in terms of visuals, McKuin did want to pay tribute to Ojai's thriving and eclectic arts scene. She shopped pieces one at a time, letting textured accents such as multimedia artwork and handcrafted furniture land where they may, creating spaces that feel as though they came together organically (which they did). Today, McKuin and her brood are living in what can only be described as a material world, with a vibe as rugged and sun-drenched as the mountains that stretch out just beyond their windows. ∎

ARTWORK SITTING ON THE FLOOR CREATES A CASUAL VIBE.

FIR COAT
For enhanced warmth in the bedrooms, McKuin ditched the concrete floors of the main living spaces in favor of Douglas-fir planks. A graphic Moroccan rug adds more softness underfoot.

ROCK STAR

Construction of the home took 18 months and required extensive excavation. Not one to let a good thing go to waste, McKuin utilized the upturned rubble to construct a guesthouse with a gabion wall system.

WISHBONE CHAIRS ADD STYLE WITHOUT BULK.

FARMHOUSE FAVORITE
TELESCOPING DOORS PROVIDE THE ULTIMATE INDOOR/OUTDOOR ENVIRONMENT.

FARMHOUSE FAVORITE
A MURPHY BED IS AN OLD-FASHIONED WAY TO ACCOMMODATE GUESTS ON THE FLY.

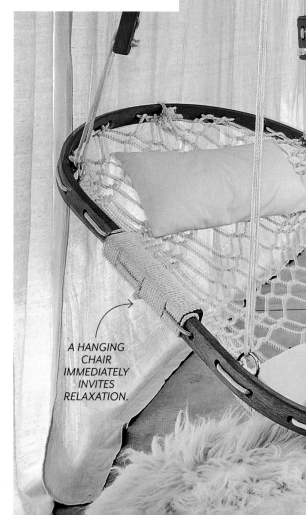

▲

MULTITASKER
With the inclusion of a Murphy bed (top pic) and easy-to-move furniture (that coffee table is on wheels), the guesthouse easily transitions from poolside hangout to overnight sleeping quarters.

▲

INSIDE OUT
McKuin continued the gabion wall into the bathroom as a visual means of connecting the streamlined washroom to the outdoors.

A HANGING CHAIR IMMEDIATELY INVITES RELAXATION.

NATURAL SHADE
For privacy from the main house, the
far bank of windows was lined with
a climbing vine that also helps to
block out early-morning sunlight.

189

POOL TIME

Just as the house was planned to feel at one with the elements, the saltwater swimming pool was designed to blend with both the house and the terrain. Wispy grasses and olive trees give it a natural finish.

FARMHOUSE FAVORITE
NATURAL GRASSES PROVIDE LANDSCAPING THAT FEELS ANYTHING BUT FORMAL.

> " We owned the property for 10 years, staying in a vintage Airstream on the weekends. That time informed how we now use our dream house."
>
> SHERRY McKUIN

JUST RIGHT

This tiny home is located amid
5 scenic acres on Oregon's
Sauvie Island. Jessica Helgerson
and her husband, Yianni,
renovated the home while
retaining the original footprint.

SMALL
WONDER

Think all farmhouses are sprawling, can-sleep-a-crowd structures? Think again! This tiny Oregon home packs farmhouse appeal into every inch of its mere 540 square feet.

THE NEW FRONT PORCH WAS BUILT AROUND A NATIVE PLUM TREE.

▼

TOPPED OFF

As part of the remodel, the home's worn-out shingles were replaced with a rooftop garden. Planted with moss and ferns that the family gathered along the Columbia River Gorge, the living roof offers year-round insulation and gives the simple white cottage a storybook quality.

It was supposed to be a vacation home. But in a single weekend, designer Jessica Helgerson's little country cottage became her family's permanent residence. "The first time we stayed the night was over Memorial Day weekend—four years ago," says Jessica. "We instantly felt so at home, we never left." The decision surprised everyone, especially Jessica, who had purchased the home as part of 5 pastoral acres on Oregon's Sauvie Island. The property, located 20 minutes from Portland, was pristine—but the house was in shambles. Rather than scrap it altogether, Jessica decided to give it a top-to-bottom overhaul. "It's had a

SIT AND STAY

Jessica originally planned to outfit the living room with four armchairs, but ultimately opted for modular built-in sofas wide enough to be used as guest beds. She credits the design switch with making the house a full-time, year-round home, especially since the family includes young children. The roomy design offered far more space for kicking up your feet with kids than the four chairs ever would. Creating a focal point in the room are custom bookshelves inherited from Jessica's father, an English professor.

195

COZY KITCHEN

Jessica didn't have to look far for building materials; the home's walls, ceiling and kitchen cabinets were crafted from wood found in one of several old barns on the property. The vintage electric range, on the other hand, required a 10-hour drive to northern California to purchase it from a Craigslist seller. Rounding out the space is a handsome walnut dining table (built by Jessica's husband, Yianni) and an assortment of midcentury modern chairs.

> 66
> This house has had a lot of lives. It felt wrong to discard something with so much history."
>
> JESSICA HELGERSON

A PANELED RANGE
HOOD ADDS
RUSTIC TEXTURE.

197

lot of lives," she explains of the circa-1940s structure, which was originally part of Portland's Zanport Village and then floated down the river to its current spot, where it became a goose-hunting check station and later a rental house. "It felt wrong to discard something with that much history." So Jessica set out to reconfigure the interior with an efficient open floor plan that would comfortably accommodate her, husband Yianni, and their children, Max and Penelope.

Out went the old nylon carpeting and worn-out sheetrock; in came wide-plank oak floors and white-paneled walls. To maximize the home's natural light, new, larger windows were installed. When it came to decor, Jessica adhered to a less-is-more approach, ensuring room for key pieces such as a rough-hewn farmhouse dining table and roomy built-in sofas. The result: an airy, inviting abode that makes you want to sit and stay a while. Years, in fact. ■

ADD PLUG-IN SCONCES TO INSTANTLY UP A ROOM'S AMBIENCE.

▶

UP ABOVE

Along this side of the house, the ceiling was taken to the rafters to make way for a sleeping loft. The compact area comfortably accommodates a king-size mattress. Patterned textiles and a vintage Moroccan rug enhance the cozy factor.

◀

ROOM FOR TWO

Efficiency abounds in the kids' bunk room, where the simple shiplap paneling conceals—surprise!—a pull-out closet at the foot of the beds. The space was too narrow for a traditional closet and door, but handily houses a clothes rod and drawers on a sliding track.

BATH TIME!
The soaking tub, a lucky hand-me-down from friends doing their own renovation, perfectly fits in the bathroom's narrow footprint. The curvy find originally boasted opulent golden feet, which Jessica replaced with wood slabs to better suit the cottage's rough-hewn aesthetic. A sheer curtain panel provides just enough privacy and beautifully filters the abundant natural light.

FARMHOUSE FAVORITE
SOAKING TUBS BRING OLD-SCHOOL STYLE TO ANY BATHROOM.

199

MAKE IT YOURS

Fun DIY projects help complete the look.

ALL ABOUT
SHIPLAP

*Consider this your go-to guide to
the quintessential farmhouse finish.*

What It Is

Don't let the name fool you!
Shiplap has rustic, not nautical roots.
The wooden board style originated
in constructing barns, sheds and country
homes. Traditional shiplap has a rabbet
(or groove) cut into the top and the bottom
of each board, which allows the pieces to fit
together snugly for a tight seal. The
gap between the two boards gives
the look eye-pleasing depth.

LINE UP
Shiplap offers a timeless
appeal by adding both texture
and clean lines to any space.

AU NATUREL
Untouched (no stain, no sanding!) boards give shiplap a rustic, cabin-ready finish.

How to Install It...

STEP 1 Pick Your Paneling
Measure the wall(s) to determine how much wood you'll need. Thanks to its current popularity, shiplap boards now come in a variety of finishes and lengths. For a preprimed version, try: Pre-Primed Radiata Pine Nickel Gap Shiplap Board, available at stores like Home Depot.

STEP 2 Prep Your Space
Remove trim moldings from wall. Sand down any raised areas that may cause an uneven finish.

STEP 3 Map It Out
Using a stud finder, mark the locations with a pencil. Then mark a floor-to-ceiling grid along those stud lines. Also, remeasure the wall to determine your preferred length of boards; cut accordingly.

STEP 4 Bring On the Boards
Starting at the bottom of the wall, add boards along the floor line. (Make sure this first pass of boards is completely level.) To ensure pieces fit snugly, use a rubber hammer to gently tap the shiplap into place before fastening to the wall. Use a nail gun to adhere the groove portion of the board to the wall, then add another nail to the board itself. Work your way across the wall from left to right, bottom to top.

STEP 5 Top It Off
After affixing boards, run your hands over the paneling to identify any spots that may be loose or ill-fitting. Tighten with additional nails.

Fake It Till You Make It! Want to save time and money? Instead of real-deal shiplap, use plywood strips instead. While these won't have the snug fit of shiplap boards, they will give you that iconic shadow line to create a convincing faux finish.

FARMHOUSE FAVORITE *A MIX OF WINDOW SIZES AND STYLES ADD BOTH LIGHT AND DIMENSION TO ANY ROOM.*

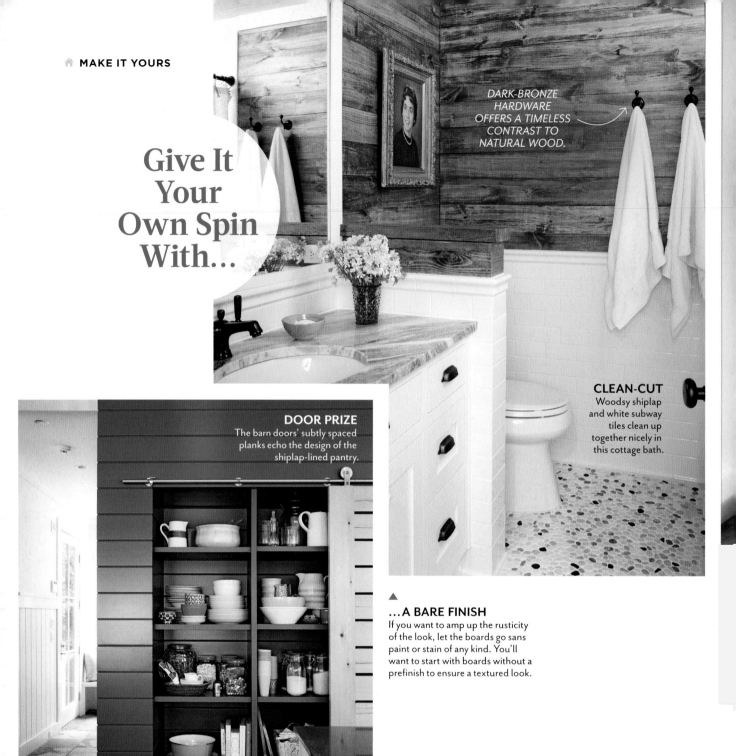

Give It Your Own Spin With…

DARK-BRONZE HARDWARE OFFERS A TIMELESS CONTRAST TO NATURAL WOOD.

CLEAN-CUT
Woodsy shiplap and white subway tiles clean up together nicely in this cottage bath.

DOOR PRIZE
The barn doors' subtly spaced planks echo the design of the shiplap-lined pantry.

…A BARE FINISH
If you want to amp up the rusticity of the look, let the boards go sans paint or stain of any kind. You'll want to start with boards without a prefinish to ensure a textured look.

…A COLORFUL COAT OF PAINT
White shiplap is the farmhouse standard, but it's certainly not the only hue worthy of the treatment. For a more modern take, consider coating the woodwork in an unexpected shade, such as the navy blue shown here.

FEELING GROOVY
A touch of drywall provides an easy-on-the-eyes break between the vertical and horizontal shiplap planks.

FARMHOUSE FAVORITE
A NATURAL FIBER, LIKE THE SISAL RUG SHOWN HERE, COMPLEMENTS THE TEXTURE OF SHIPLAP WALLS.

...A UNIQUE ORIENTATION
Horizontal is the traditional shiplap layout, but the charm doesn't have to stop there. Accentuate the height of a tall space with a vertical display, or manipulate scale by lining up ceiling and wall boards in opposite directions.

COUNTRY COUSINS
Get to know these other farmhouse-approved varieties of millwork.

Beadboard
Features narrow wood planks lined vertically on the wall. In between each is an even narrower indentation—also known as a bead.

Board and Batten
Flat, wide boards affixed to the wall, with narrow wooden strips, called battens, covering seams between boards.

V-Groove
Also called tongue-and-groove, this style uses boards with deep-angled edges that come together to create a "V" shape when affixed to one another.

FOREVER IN
BLUE JEANS

Add laid-back style with projects crafted from salvaged denim.

The Project
JEAN POCKET POUCHES
Give your walls a cheeky lift.

FARMHOUSE FAVORITE
NOTHING SAYS AMERICANA LIKE AN ODE TO OLD GLORY CRAFTED FROM FADED DENIM.

The Project
FADED BLUE FLAG
Create an all-American focal point.

TURN WORN-OUT WARDROBE STAPLES INTO RIVETING DÉCOR!

DENIM RAG RUG

What You'll Need
- Plastic canvas mesh (1/4-inch mesh)
- Fabric scissors
- Denim jeans or other denim clothing (the more worn the better)
- Crochet hook (optional)

What You'll Do

STEP 1 Unroll the mesh and cut to the size you want your rug to be.

STEP 2 Cut denim into strips 1 to 2 inches wide and 4 to 6 inches long. Don't worry about including hemmed edges; these can easily be worked into the design.

STEP 3 Insert a denim strip into one hole in mesh and pull it back through the next hole (a crochet hook makes this easier). Tie it firmly in place. Repeat until all sections of the mesh are covered and there are no gaps that show through to the floor.

JEAN POCKET POUCHES

What You'll Need
- Tape measure
- Tailor's chalk
- Denim jeans (one back pocket per pouch)
- Fabric scissors
- Embroidery hoop (9 to 12 inches should fit most pockets). You'll need one hoop per pouch.

What You'll Do

STEP 1 Using a tape measure and tailor's chalk, draw a circle at least 2 inches larger than your embroidery hoop around the back pocket of a pair of jeans. (Most dinner plates will make a good template.) Cut out the circle with sharp fabric scissors and set aside.

STEP 2 Unscrew or separate the embroidery hoop into two hoops. Place the smaller hoop on a flat surface and put the denim fabric circle neatly on top so the pocket sits squarely in the middle.

STEP 3 Place the larger hoop on top; screw the hoop securely in place so it holds the fabric taut. Trim away any excess denim from around the edges.

STEP 4 Hang pouch using a small nail or adhesive hook.

FADED BLUE FLAG

What You'll Need
- Denim jeans in varying washes
- Fabric scissors
- Denim-weight thread in blue
- Sewing machine
- Grommets and grommet press (optional; to make eyelets for displaying flag)

What You'll Do

STEP 1 Plan dimensions of flag. For info on American flag proportions, visit chamberofcommerce.org

STEP 2 Cut off jeans 2 inches below the belt line. Sort waist sections into light and dark washes.

STEP 3 Stitch like colors together end to end using denim thread and a sewing machine. Cut strips to flag length.

STEP 4 Line up strips, alternating dark and light to make the flag's field. Stitch together.

STEP 5 Using darker scraps, cut a large rectangle for the canton (star field) and stitch it to the upper left corner of the flag. Cut stars out of light-wash scraps and glue to canton.

USE CRAFT STORE STAPLES (LIKE THIS EMBROIDERY HOOP) TO GIVE JEANS NEW FORM AND FUNCTION.

211

DIY
PAINT
PROJECTS

*This expert-backed primer will have
you on a roll, with ideas big and small.*

How to Paint...CABINETS

MAKE A MARK Cabinetry is easier to paint when the hinges and fronts are removed. But that can also mean a lot of miscellaneous pieces floating around your work space if items aren't properly inventoried. For an orderly process, write the location ("left cabinet over fridge" for example) on the upper right-hand side of the back of each door. (You can leave this part unpainted until the very end.) Place hardware in individual plastic bags with the same labels.

LIFT UP There's nothing worse than painting an item and then having it stick to your drop cloth. (Peeling paint, anyone?) Avoid that midproject headache by placing the cabinet fronts on sawhorses or painter's pyramids—both are available at local hardware stores.

How to Paint...STAIRS

LIGHTEN THE LOAD It's hard enough to tote paint up and down a ladder. But with stairs, forget about it! Eschew a gallon bucket or full-size paint pan in favor of a handheld cup or small roller tray. Your arms (and steps) will thank you.

SKIP IT If you need to access the upstairs during the project, start by painting every other step so you can go up and down on dry treads as needed. If access is not an issue, start at the top of the stairwell and work your way down. You're less likely to spoil wet paint with this orientation.

COME UP SHORT If you're planning a design on the stair treads, map out the look with painter's tape. Avoid the urge to roll out long strips and instead, use short ones—they will be easier to apply and will pull up without tangles.

PROS ADVISE REMOVING ALL HARDWARE BEFORE PAINTING.

How to Paint... **TRIM**

TAKE NOTE To ensure you get the most out of a fresh coat, invest some time into filling any cracks or imperfections before you paint. You'll easily spot these by running a small flashlight along the material; use a pencil to circle any areas that need attention.

LEAD THE WAY If you're painting an entire room (walls and all), start with the trim—it will be easier to tape off than the wall itself.

PAINT, SAND, REPEAT For an impossibly smooth and glossy finish, sand the trim (a fine-grit sanding sponge will offer the best results) between coats. Vacuum up any dust before applying the next layer of paint.

How to Paint... **A BATHTUB**

KEEP IT SUPERFICIAL Painting an antique claw-foot tub (or a new one, for that matter) is a low-effort project with a seriously high yield. Just be sure to keep the paint on the outside of the tub only. The inside should remain glazed cast iron or ceramic to ensure proper water safety.

PREP RIGHT Before applying your pretty new shade, thoroughly clean the tub's exterior and then coat with a metal primer for a durable finish. For the best application, apply with a foam roller.

How to Paint... **A FRONT DOOR**

FILL UP Before painting, treat any nicks with wood filler to ensure a smooth, finished product. After all, nothing makes a good first impression quite like a beautiful front door!

RISE AND PRIME Start with an exterior-grade primer, which will help protect it from the elements.

GET DOWN For best results, paint the door while it's off its hinges. Plan to start early so you can apply primer and multiple coats of paint—and have time to let them all dry—before nightfall.

FARMHOUSE FAVORITE
A GRAPHIC WALLPAPER MAKES A STYLISH COMPANION TO PAINTED TRIM.

215

How to Paint... FLOORS

CHOOSE WISELY Because floors come in contact with shoes, furniture, and the like, not just any paint will do. For ultimate durability, choose a marine-grade paint, which will give treads a coat that's both hearty and waterproof.

PICK SIDES Whether you're doing a single color or a fun design like the one shown here, be sure to start your project in one corner of the room and work your way out and across from there. This strategy will prevent streaks and drips in already completed areas.

WAIT IT OUT To avoid mucking up your handiwork, make sure floors have not just dried but properly cured (all solvents have evaporated and the surface has completely hardened) before placing furniture and rugs. The curing process can take anywhere from two days to a full month—check with the paint manufacturer to confirm the time frame.

FARMHOUSE FAVORITE
THE MORE ORNATE THE FLOOR PATTERN, THE SIMPLER THE WALL TREATMENT SHOULD BE.

How to Paint… FURNITURE

WEAR IT DOWN If you only ever sand during one paint project, let it be with furniture. Due to most pieces' many planes and angles, this process can take some time. But a thorough prep will ensure a cohesive and peel-resistant finished product.

FLIP OUT (AND OVER) As with sanding, painting furniture is a time-intensive endeavor, if only because of the many visible surfaces. Turn your piece on its back, side and bottom to guarantee a comprehensive coat.

REMEMBER, LESS IS MORE Plan on three or four thin coats of satin paint for an even finish. A heavy first coat might be satisfying, but it will lead to a less-professional look.

BLACK CHALKBOARD PAINT WILL INSTANTLY DRESS UP A DATED FRIDGE.

How to Paint… AN APPLIANCE

TAKE IT OUTSIDE Moving a heavy appliance like a stove or refrigerator is certainly no easy task; it means hauling a large item and disconnecting any of its electrical or water lines. But most appliance-grade paints (epoxy-based formulas that are flame-resistant) pack quite an odor until they dry. For safety around the fumes, do your painting outdoors.

STICK TOGETHER If you'd like your appliance to be magnetic (hello, fun pictures and cute drawings on the fridge!), cover the item with a magnetic primer, available in spray paint form at hardware stores.

HAVE YOUR EYE ON THE PRIZE Luckily, you can save time with an appliance by painting just the portions that will be visible once the item is finally put back into its original location. The sides of stoves and refrigerators often boast the largest amount of surface area, but in reality they will usually go unseen from day to day once they are tucked back into their proper spots.

217

CREDITS

COVER Casey Dunn **2–3** Sean Gallagher Photography **4–5** Rikki Snyder; Brian Austin/Michael Kaskel; Mark Lohman; TI Media Limited/David Giles **6–7** Doug Peterson Photography **8–9** Anthony Crisafulli **10–11** Gaffer Photography **12–13** Muffy Kibbery; Eric Roth (2); Sean Gallagher **14–15** Paul Varney Construction; Troy Thies; Twist Tours; Susan Teare Photography **16–23** GAP Interiors/Mark Ashbee; Anthony Crisafulli; GAP Interiors/Robin Stubbert; GAP Interiors/David Giles; GAP Interiors/David Giles; GAP Interiors/David Giles; GAP Interiors/Bureaux; GAP Interiors/Bureaux; Eric Roth; OTTO Archive/David A. Land; *Product images supplied by vendors:* Big Chill Appliances, Caitlin Wilson, Cost Plus World Market, Vintage Brass Lights, Moroccan Tile Shop (Etsy), Faux Wood Beams, Online Fabric Store **24–27** OTTO Archive/David A. Land; OTTO Archive/David Tsay; OTTO Archive/Eric Piasecki; TI Media Limited/Simon Bevan; *Product images supplied by vendors:* Murray Feiss Lighting, Flower Muse, The Home Depot, Bed Bath and Beyond, Gum Drop Lane, Pottery Barn, Amazon, Wayfair, Roostery, Walmart, Sam's Club, Get Back Inc., Rove and Swig, R. C. Willey, Kaufman Mercantile, Rejuvenation **28–29** GAP Interiors/House & Leisure (D. Ross); GAP Interiors/Bureaux (Greg Cox); GAP Interiors (Nick Carter); GAP Interiors (Jonathan Gooch) **30–31** GAP Interiors (Tria Giovan); GAP Interiors (Colin Poole); GAP Interiors (Nick Carter) **32–33** Michael Kaskel **34–41** Tim Cuppett Architects **42–55** Raquel Langworthy **56–69** Brian Austin; Michael Kaskel **70–83** Rikki Snyder **84–95** Lissa Gotwals **96–101** Casey Dunn **102–113** Genius Bar: Costa Christ Media **114–123** Becki Griffin **124–135** Mark Lohman **136–145** James Solomon **146–155** OTTO Archive/Lisa Romerein **156–163** OTTO/Paul Costello **164–177** Karyn Millet **178–191** Sherri J Photography **192–199** Lincoln Barbour **200–201** OTTO Archive/David A. Land **202–203** poligonchik/Getty Images; OTTO Archive/Lisa Romerein **204–205** Breadmaker/Shutterstock **206–207** OTTO Archive/David A. Land; OTTO Archive/ Lisa Romerein; All products courtesy of Manufacturer **208–211** TI Media Limited/David Giles; TI Media Limited/David Giles; GAP Interiors/Costas Picadas; Getty Images/Mehmet Hilmi Barcin; Getty Images/Geografika **212–217** OTTO Archive (David A. Land); OTTO Archive (David A. Land); OTTO Archive (Lisa Romerein); GAP Interiors (David Cleaveland); OTTO Archive (Paul Costello); OTTO Archive (Trevor Tondro); OTTO Archive (Lisa Romerein); OTTO Archive (Lisa Romerein) **BACK COVER** Corey Gaffer Photography

CENTENNIAL BOOKS

An Imprint of
Centennial Media, LLC
40 Worth St., 10th Floor
New York, NY 10013, U.S.A.

ISBN 978-1-951274-60-3

Distributed by
Simon & Schuster, Inc.
1230 Avenue of the Americas
New York, NY 10020, U.S.A.

For information about custom editions, special sales and premium and corporate purchases, please contact Centennial Media at contact@centennialmedia.com.

Manufactured in China

Publishers & Co-Founders Ben Harris, Sebastian Raatz
Editorial Director Annabel Vered
Creative Director Jessica Power
Executive Editor Janet Giovanelli
Features Editor Alyssa Shaffer
Deputy Editors Ron Kelly, Anne Marie O'Connor
Design Director Martin Elfers
Senior Art Director Pino Impastato
Art Directors Olga Jakim, Natali Suasnavas, Joseph Ulatowski
Copy/Production Patty Carroll, Angela Taormina
Assistant Art Director Jaclyn Loney
Photo Editor Jenny Veiga
Production Manager Paul Rodina
Production Assistant Alyssa Swiderski
Editorial Assistant Tiana Schippa
Sales & Marketing Jeremy Nurnberg